CHARACTERS

A one-year exploration of the Bible
through the lives of its people.

VOLUME FOUR

The Prophets

LifeWay Press® • Nashville, Tennessee

EDITORIAL TEAM

Brandon Hiltibidal
Director, Discipleship and Groups Ministry

Brian Daniel
Manager, Short-Term Discipleship

Joel Polk
Editorial Team Leader

Mike Livingstone
Content Developer

David Briscoe
Content Developer

G.B. Howell Jr.
Content Developer

Rob Tims
Content Editor

Laura Magness
Content Editor

Gena Rogers
Production Editor

Darin Clark
Art Director

Denise Wells
Designer

Lauren Rives
Designer

From the creators of *Explore the Bible, Explore the Bible: Characters* is a seven-volume resource that examines the lives of biblical characters within the historical, cultural, and biblical context of Scripture. Each six-session volume includes videos to help your group understand the way each character fits into the storyline of the Bible.

© 2020 LifeWay Press®

ISBN 978-1-4300-7038-2 • Item 005823506
Dewey decimal classification: 220.92
Subject headings: BIBLE. O.T.--BIOGRAPHY / BIBLE. O.T. PROPHETS

We believe that the Bible has God for its author; salvation for its end; and truth, without any mixture of error, for its matter and that all Scripture is totally true and trustworthy. To review LifeWay's doctrinal guideline, please visit lifeway.com/doctrinalguideline.

Scripture quotations are taken from the Christian Standard Bible®, Copyright © 2017 by Holman Bible Publishers. Used by permission. Christian Standard Bible® and CSB® are federally registered trademarks of Holman Bible Publishers.

To order additional copies of this resource, write to LifeWay Resources Customer Service; One LifeWay Plaza; Nashville, TN 37234; fax 615-251-5933; call toll free 800-458-2772; or order online at LifeWay.com; email orderentry@lifeway.com.

Printed in the United States of America

Groups Ministry Publishing • LifeWay Resources
One LifeWay Plaza • Nashville, TN 37234

CONTENTS

ABOUT EXPLORE THE BIBLE

The Whole Truth, Book by Book

Explore the Bible is an ongoing family of Bible study resources that guides the whole church through the only source of the truth on which we can rely: God's Word. Each session frames Scripture with biblical and historical context vital to understanding its original intent, and unpacks the transforming truth of God's Word in a manner that is practical, age-appropriate, and repeatable over a lifetime.

Find out more at goExploreTheBible.com.

HOW TO USE THIS STUDY

This Bible study includes six sessions of content for group and personal study. Regardless of what day of the week your group meets, each session begins with group study. Each group session utilizes the following elements to facilitate simple yet meaningful interaction among group members and with God's Word.

INTRODUCTION
This page includes introductory content and questions to get the conversation started each time your group meets.

GROUP DISCUSSION
Each session has a corresponding teaching video to introduce the story. These videos have been created specifically to teach the group more about the biblical figure being studied. After watching the video, continue the group discussion by reading the Scripture passages and discussing the questions that follow. Finally, conclude each group session with a time of prayer, reflecting on what you discussed.

BIOGRAPHY AND FURTHER INSIGHT MOMENT
These sections provide more in-depth information regarding the biblical character being spotlighted each session and can be included in the group discussion or personal study times.

PERSONAL STUDY
Three personal studies are provided for each session to take individuals deeper into Scripture and to supplement the content introduced in the group study. With biblical teaching and introspective questions, these sections challenge individuals to grow in their understanding of God's Word and to respond in faith.

LEADER GUIDE
A tear out leader guide for each session is provided on pages 95-106. This section also includes sample answers or discussion prompts to help you jump start or steer the conversation.

VOLUME FOUR

The Prophets

ELIJAH
The Bold Prophet

INTRODUCTION

The ministry of Elijah is set against the background of King Ahab's rule in Israel. Ahab reigned in the ninth century BC and was Israel's worst king in many ways. He married a foreign wife, Jezebel, who was a devoted follower of Baal and determined to make Baal worship the official state religion of Israel. The Israelites increasingly mixed Baal worship with their worship of the Lord. Further, God's prophets were forced into hiding when Jezebel started slaughtering them.

In that chaotic context, Elijah determined to challenge the king and people to decide once and for all whom they would serve—either the Lord or Baal. His stand on Mount Carmel marks the decisive moment when allegiance to Yahweh and allegiance to Baal met in a head-on clash.

In Elijah, we see a man who took a bold stand for the Lord. More importantly, we see a powerful God whose presence and encouragement are available to us when we take bold stands for Him.

When have you taken what you would consider to be a bold stand for the Lord?

In what ways did you experience God's presence and encouragement during that time?

Watch the video teaching for Session 1 to discover "The World of Elijah," then continue the group discussion.

Focus Attention

Elijah withstood the pressure to compromise his personal convictions. Describe a time when you felt pressured to conform in order to "fit in." How did you respond?

Explore The Text

As a group, read 1 Kings 18:17-21.

If a modern-day Elijah was speaking to our culture, how do you think he might express his challenge in verse 21?

Why didn't the people say anything in response to Elijah's challenge?

As a group, read 1 Kings 18:22-24.

What was Elijah hoping to accomplish by establishing the contest with the prophets of Baal?

What does Elijah's challenge to the prophets of Baal say about the nature of faith?

As a group, read 1 Kings 18:25-29.

What actions did the prophets of Baal take to try to persuade their god to send fire? What additional insights about the nature of faith do we learn from their actions?

As a group, read 1 Kings 18:36-39.

How did Elijah's prayer contrast with the prayers of the prophets of Baal? What is significant about this?

Does God answer prayers today like He did those of Elijah? Should we expect God's miraculous intervention as was shown in Elijah's situation?

APPLY THE TEXT

Elijah took a bold stand for the Lord as he confronted the worship of false gods in his day. Unlike the prophets of Baal, Elijah had a personal relationship with the living God that infused him with strength, integrity, and the ability to take an unpopular stand. Most of us will never be called on to take a stand as dramatic as the one taken by Elijah, but we are all given opportunities to stand up for our beliefs and for the truths of God's Word. As we take bold stands for the Lord, we can count on His continuing presence and encouragement.

What's the main point of the story—what Elijah did for God or what God did through Elijah? Why does it matter that we understand the difference?

When you are confronted with differing viewpoints about God, what do you tend to do? What would it mean for you to follow Elijah's example?

How can the story of Elijah encourage and prepare you for the time when the Lord asks you to do something that will require a bold step of faith?

Close your group time in prayer, reflecting on what you have discussed.

ELIJAH

KEY VERSE

Then Elijah approached all the people and said, "How long will you waver between two opinions? If the LORD is God, follow him. But if Baal, follow him." But the people didn't answer him a word.

— 1 Kings 18:21

BASIC FACTS

1. A powerful prophet of the Lord to the Northern Kingdom of Israel during the reigns of King Ahab and his son and successor, Ahaziah.

2. Name *Elijah* means "my God is Yahweh (the Lord)."

3. A resident of Tishbe in Gilead, a region that lay southeast of the Sea of Galilee on the eastern side of the Jordan River.

4. Lived a rustic lifestyle in wilderness areas, yet appeared in the palaces of kings to deliver prophetic messages from the Lord.

5. Did not die but was taken up into heaven in a whirlwind by the Lord.

TIMELINE

900–850 BC

- First temple reform under Asa 897
- Omri (Israel) makes Samaria his capital 880
- Ahab reigns in Northern Kingdom 874–853
- Jehoshaphat rules in Judah 872–848
- Elijah's prophetic ministry 862–852
- Shalmaneser III becomes king in Assyria 859
- Ben-hadad (Syria) attacks Samaria 857

850–800 BC

- Elisha's prophetic ministry 850–798
- Athaliah's reign of terror in Judah 841–835
- Jehu's reign in Northern Kingdom 841–814
- Joel's prophetic ministry (early date) 836–796
- Second temple reform under Joash 812

KNOWN FOR

1. Elijah announced a three-year drought God sent in judgment against the wickedness of King Ahab of Israel. During the drought, God miraculously provided for Elijah through a poor widow in the town of Zarephath. Elijah later raised back to life the widow's son who had died suddenly (1 Kings 17).

2. Elijah challenged 450 prophets of Baal on Mount Carmel to prove their god's existence and power. When they could not, Elijah called on the Lord to manifest His power through fire, which the Lord did (1 Kings 18:20-39).

3. Ahab's Canaanite queen, Jezebel, put out a death decree against Elijah, leading to the prophet's fearful flight southward to the wilderness and Mount Horeb. There the prophet was fed by ravens and received the Lord's soft voice of encouragement and instruction, directing Elijah to anoint both King Ahab's successors as well as his own (1 Kings 19).

4. Elijah confronted King Ahab and Jezebel for stealing Naboth's ancestral land (and vineyard) by having the man murdered. Elijah prophesied the king and queen would be killed for their evil deeds (1 Kings 21).

5. Having anointed Elisha as his successor, Elijah was taken up to heaven in a whirlwind (2 Kings 2:1-12).

6. Elijah appeared alongside Moses and talked with Jesus at Jesus' transfiguration (Matt. 17:1-4).

800–750 BC

- Uzziah reigns in Judah 794–740
- First Olympic Games held in Greece 776
- Jonah's prophetic ministry 770
- First documented solar eclipse in Assyria 763

750–700 BC

- Isaiah's prophetic ministry 742–700
- Tiglath-pileser III rules in Assyria 745–727
- Syro-Ephraimite war against Judah 735
- Northern Kingdom conquered by Assyria 722
- Hezekiah rules in Judah 715–686
- Sennacherib (Assyria) invades Judah 701

Elijah: A Man of God

By Robert C. Dunston

The Bible refers several times to Elijah as a "man of God" (see 1 Kings 17:24; 2 Kings 1:9-13) placing him in the company of faithful individuals like Moses (Deut. 33:1), Samuel (1 Sam. 9:6-10), David (2 Chron. 8:14), and Elisha (2 Kings 4:7,22). Elijah's ministry occurred during the reigns of Ahab (874–853 BC) and Ahaziah (853–852 BC), both kings of the Northern Kingdom.

Ahab married Jezebel, a princess from the Phoenician city of Tyre. He allowed Jezebel to worship her pagan gods; he built a temple in Samaria to Baal and set up an Asherah pole (1 Kings 16:31-33). Having freedom of worship and a place to worship were not enough for Jezebel. She became an evangelist for her god Baal, actively seeking to lead the Israelites to worship him rather than God; she killed those who opposed her. Baal's followers worshiped him as the storm god who brought rains (and thus fertility) to the land; he supposedly provided for the people's agricultural needs.

Most of Elijah's ministry focused on combating belief in Baal and trying to bring Israel's leaders and people back to exclusive faith in God. In Elijah's initial confrontation with Ahab, Elijah prophesied that God would withhold rain and dew for the next several years. While Ahab blamed the drought on Elijah, the prophet explained the drought was God's punishment for Ahab and Jezebel leading the Israelites to worship Baal (1 Kings 18:17-18).

The climactic showdown occurred on Mount Carmel, when Elijah challenged the 450 prophets of Baal and the 400 prophets of Asherah to see whether Baal or God could provide fire to consume a sacrifice (1 Kings 18:20-39). While the prophets of Baal, despite their efforts, received no response from their god, God sent fire from heaven to consume the sacrifice, wood, altar, and water. The people professed their loyalty to the Lord.

Elijah's final conflict with Baal worship involved King Ahab's son and successor Ahaziah. After accidentally injuring himself, Ahaziah sent messengers to inquire of Baal-zebub, a Philistine god, whether he would recover. Elijah intercepted the messengers and told them Ahaziah's consulting a foreign god rather than the Lord had doomed him (2 Kings 1:1-6).

Overlooking Ajloun, Jordan, from Mar Elias, which tradition holds to be Tishbe, the hometown of Elijah.

With the Jordan River Valley in the background, observation deck at the site where the prophet Elijah is said to have ascended into heaven.

Illustrator Photo/ Brent Bruce (60-8010)
Illustrator Photo/ Brent Bruce (60-8075)

Elijah also demanded justice in Israel. When Ahab and Jezebel engineered Naboth's death so they could seize his vineyard, Elijah confronted Ahab and pronounced God's judgment on him and Jezebel (see 1 Kings 21).

Even a "man of God" can experience despair. After God's victory on Mount Carmel, Elijah fled in terror from Jezebel's wrath, complaining to God that he was the only faithful person left and asking to die (1 Kings 19:3-8). God cared for Elijah and responded to his prayers by providing food, His presence, and new tasks. When Elijah completed his ministry, God brought His prophet home not through death, but through a miraculous transition that Elijah's successor Elisha witnessed (2 Kings 2:11-12). Elijah left behind an enduring legacy and example of what a man of God can accomplish.

Robert C. Dunston, "Elijah: A Man of God," *Biblical Illustrator*, Winter 2010-11.

Read 1 Kings 17:1-24.

Ahab reigned for twenty-two years and proved to be the most ungodly king Israel ever had. His wife Jezebel led him in embracing the worship of Baal and attempting to make Baal worship the official religion of Israel.

In 1 Kings 17, the Lord sent the prophet Elijah to call Ahab and the nation back to Him. The message Elijah delivered to Ahab was ominous. The land of Israel would experience a long-term drought until God decreed that the rains come again (see v. 1). Elijah's prediction of drought marked a direct challenge to worshipers of Baal who believed their god exercised control over rain, wind, and clouds.

Ahab recognized Elijah's prophecy as a direct affront to Baalism. Neither Ahab nor Jezebel would tolerate such treasonous words against their new national religion. To protect Elijah, the Lord directed him to hide in a ravine east of the Jordan River, where God miraculously cared for the prophet. Each morning and evening ravens flew to Elijah, bringing bread and meat; the water flowing in the ravine brought him drink (vv. 2-4).

The Lord sent Elijah to Zarephath in Sidon, a center of Baal worship. This is noteworthy because Jezebel came from Sidon, where her father ruled as king. The prophet would live in the heart of a land dominated by Baalism. Yet before Elijah arrived, God was at work preparing the heart of a widow to receive both His prophet and a miracle. The Lord commanded the widow to provide for Elijah with her last bit of food. She had intended to prepare a last meal of bread for herself and her son, then wait to die of starvation.

God commanded Elijah to go to Zarephath, a center of Baal worship, where a widow would provide for him. Do you think those instructions made sense to Elijah at the time? What lessons can we learn from this?

Elijah urged the widow not to be afraid, then asked her to do something incredibly difficult: make bread for him first, then some for her son and herself (v. 13). If the widow followed Elijah's instructions, God would ensure that her jar of flour and jug of oil would never be empty until God brought rain back to the land (v. 14).

Elijah asked the widow to take a step of faith. What step of faith is God asking you to take?

On hearing God's promise, the widow believed and obeyed. God responded to her faithful action by keeping His promise. As long as the drought lasted, Elijah, the woman, and her son had enough to eat (vv. 15-16).

Later, the widow's son became ill and died. Calling Elijah a "man of God" (v. 18), the widow accused him of punishing her for her sin. She probably assumed that the illness and death meant God was punishing her for some wrongdoing.

Elijah did not answer the woman's question. Instead, he took the boy to his room. Elijah prayed for the boy's life, and the Lord answered his prayer (vv. 19-23). The boy's death became an opportunity for God to display His love and power to a Sidonian woman in a country given over to the worship of Baal.

Once the woman saw that her son was alive, she knew Elijah was a man of God. God had done several miracles *for* Elijah. Now, He had done a miracle *through* Elijah.

What can you learn from Elijah's life about being the kind of person God uses to bless others?

For both Elijah and the widow, steps of faith involved risk. They had to act on God's promise without being able to see or even explain how everything would work out. God took care of their needs. In a world filled with uncertainty, their actions set an example for all of us.

Read 1 Kings 18:17-29,36-39.

King Ahab actively promoted Baal worship in Israel through the influence of his wife Jezebel. Followers of Baal believed their god was responsible for sending rain and providing fertile crops. Elijah, determined to demonstrate the sovereignty of the God of Israel, swore an oath promising that God would withhold the rain (1 Kings 17:1). In the third year of the drought, "The famine was severe in Samaria," and the Lord called Elijah to confront Ahab (18:2).

Ahab never understood the drought as the Lord's chastisement. Instead, he accused Elijah of being "the one ruining Israel" (v. 17). Elijah reversed that charge, pointing to Ahab's sin and calling for a contest with Jezebel's prophets of Baal (vv. 18-19). Ahab accepted Elijah's challenge, believing Baal's prophets would be victorious over Elijah. He summoned all the Israelites, just as Elijah had requested.

When might your obedience to God bring accusations from others? How will you respond to those charges?

The contest began with Elijah confronting the crowd with a question: "How long will you waver between two opinions?" (v. 21). The Hebrew word translated *waver* means "to limp." Elijah viewed the people's vacillating loyalties between the Lord and Baal as a person limping along. The "two opinions" concerned whether they believed God or Baal was the provider of rain and the soil's fertility. Apparently, the people had attempted to hedge their bets by worshiping both Yahweh and Baal. Given the intensity of Jezebel's devotion to Baal, failing to worship this idol might have been met with death. If she did not hesitate to slaughter the Lord's prophets (v. 4), she certainly would have had no reservations about killing others.

Sooner or later, each of us will find ourselves having to choose between differing opinions. Elijah demanded the Israelites stop dilly-dallying and decide whether they would serve the Lord or Baal. God's people today take a bold stand when they decisively show they follow the Lord, even when their culture is dominated by false worship.

In what area of your life are you wavering between two opinions with regard to obeying God's will? What is keeping you from total loyalty to the Lord?

Both sides placed a sacrificial bull on an altar. Elijah would call on God, and the prophets of Baal would call on their god. Whichever deity answered by consuming the offering in fire would be recognized as the one true deity. The prophets of Baal went first. They called on their god from morning to the time of evening sacrifice. Their shouts, ritual dances, and bloodletting were to no avail. Baal was a no-show.

Elijah took the counterintuitive step of drenching the altar with twelve pots of water, then began to call on the Lord (v. 36). The prophet wanted to accomplish three things. First, he wanted the people to know the Lord was God. Second, he wanted them to know he was the Lord's servant, who acted on God's word. Finally, he wanted the people to know that the Lord turned their hearts back to Him using this contest (v. 37).

God heard Elijah's prayer and completely consumed the altar and everything near it. Baal was proven a counterfeit deity. As for Elijah, God answered his prayer, because he chose to stand boldly for the Lord and trusted in God's help.

Have you ever been guilty of devoting your life to counterfeit gods—status, appearance, material possession? How do these gods help in times of crisis or desperation? How does their silence compare with the silence of Baal?

The Israelites affirmed the Lord as God when they saw how He answered Elijah's prayer. When we trust in God's help amid pressures to conform to the world, we can count on the Lord's powerful presence.

Read 1 Kings 19:1-18.

We should never expect spiritual victories and triumphs of the Lord to go unchallenged by those who do not love Him. Following the contest on Carmel (see 1 Kings 18:20-40), Ahab descended the mountain and told Jezebel everything Elijah had done. The news that he had killed all the prophets of Baal focused her destructive gaze on the prophet more intensely than ever. Apparently, the drought-ending downpour (see 18:45) did nothing to persuade Jezebel of the Lord's power or to dissuade her from believing in Baal and Asherah. Her heart was focused on revenge.

The evil queen sent a death threat against Elijah. Her oath in 1 Kings 19:2 revealed three things about her. First, Jezebel still believed in her gods in spite of the failed contest on Mount Carmel. Second, she was as committed to Baal and Asherah as Elijah was to the Lord. She felt compelled to respond to Elijah's attack on the prophets of her gods. Third, she focused her evil intentions openly on the immediate destruction of Elijah. She wanted him dead.

Elijah became afraid. Wouldn't you? The victory on Mount Carmel vanished in the heat of impending death. He panicked and ran for his life. The bold stand he had previously taken for the Lord was neutralized by his fear. Elijah needed help and encouragement.

Why do you think the Bible exposes the weaknesses of its heroes of the faith? In what ways does this encourage you?

While standing boldly for the Lord brings victory and joy, it can also lead to exhaustion and disillusionment as the battle continues. Like Elijah, we can lose heart. We need to watch for spiritual slips during these vulnerable times. Often, people are at their weakest immediately following a "mountaintop" experience.

Elijah journeyed to Horeb, the mountain of God (vv. 8-12). There, the Lord revealed His presence to Elijah then spoke softly to his prophet: "What are you doing here?" (v. 13).

Why do you think God asked Elijah this question?

The Lord then gave Elijah a threefold commission. First, he was to anoint a new king, Hazael, over Aram. Second, Elijah was to anoint a new king, Jehu, over Israel. Finally, Elijah was to anoint Elisha as a prophet in Elijah's place.

Sometimes, the best cure for feelings of hopelessness is reengagement in a worthy cause. Elijah loved the Lord and served Him faithfully. God did not discard Elijah because he went through a bout of despair. Instead, the Lord spoke softly to him and treated him graciously while seeking to restore his confidence. The Lord's assignment garnered Elijah's full attention, thus preventing him from dwelling any longer on his personal circumstances.

As the Lord continued to help Elijah climb back up, He assured the disheartened prophet he was not alone. The seven thousand faithful in Israel negated Elijah's belief that he alone was left as a faithful servant of the Lord. In this way, the Lord encouraged Elijah to get back in the fight. Elijah began his climb back by getting Elisha to join him (vv. 19-21).

What might cause you to give up in your service of God? What lessons from Elijah's story can keep you going?

By remembering we are not alone in standing boldly for the Lord, we can find strength to go about the work God has given us. The battle wages on; the Lord is looking for faithful people to charge the enemy. When we get down, let's look to the Lord, climb back on our feet, and get back into the battle.

JONAH

The Reluctant Prophet

INTRODUCTION

Many of the Old Testament prophets displayed courageous obedience to the Lord. Jonah wasn't among them—at least not initially. When the Lord called him to go take His message to another people group, Jonah rebelled.

The Lord gave Jonah a specific directive. There was absolutely no ambiguity. God told the prophet precisely what He wanted him to do: Go the city of Nineveh and preach against it. For whatever reason, the prophet decided to do the exact opposite. Rather than obey, he chose to go to a place as far away from Nineveh as possible. Jonah did not merely choose to do nothing when God presented him with this task. Rather, he actively and passionately moved in the contrary direction. Interestingly enough, he was fleeing more than Nineveh; he was trying to flee from the Lord's presence.

We all have a little bit of Jonah in us. Any one of us may be tempted to resist doing God's will if His will differs from our own desires. While some believers run from specific tasks God calls them to perform, many more simply refuse to run with God in everyday life. Fortunately, God does not quickly give up on His people who fail to do His will.

In what ways are you like Jonah?

How has God pursued you in a situation when you were resistant to do His will?

Watch the video teaching for Session 2 to discover "The World of Jonah," then continue the group discussion.

GROUP DISCUSSION

FOCUS ATTENTION

What excuses do you typically use to justify disobedience to God?

EXPLORE THE TEXT

As a group, read Jonah 1:1-3.

What was God's assignment for Jonah? How did Jonah respond?

What was Jonah trying to accomplish by fleeing to Tarshish? What do you suppose he was thinking as he boarded the ship?

As a group, read Jonah 1:4,7-12.

What's ironic about what Jonah told the sailors concerning himself and God? How did his actions and words contradict one another? Why are both actions and words important in sharing God's message?

Do you think Jonah's request to be thrown into the sea reflected God's will, or was that still Jonah being rebellious? Explain your answer.

As a group, read Jonah 1:17–2:4,9-10.

Were God's actions in verse 17 a demonstration of His judgment or His mercy? How was Jonah finally showing some sense?

As a group, read Jonah 3:1-5.

How did Jonah respond to God's command this time? What message from God did Jonah preach in Nineveh? What do you find unusual about Jonah's sermon?

As a group, read Jonah 3:10–4:11.

What was the intent of God's confronting Jonah with the question in verse 4?

How did God teach Jonah a lesson about His compassion for lost people?

APPLY THE TEXT

We are left at the end of the Book of Jonah without knowing whether the prophet changed his attitude. Because the book is open-ended, it effectively probes our attitudes about God's compassion for lost people. We don't know the end to Jonah's story, but we can know the ending to our story. We can choose to view all people groups with compassion and act on that compassion.

What lessons, good and bad, can we learn from Jonah? What attitudes prevent us from viewing all people with godly compassion?

Who are the "Ninevites" in your life? What would it take to run to them, not away from them?

If you had been Jonah, how would the story have ended? Why?

Close your group time in prayer, reflecting on what you have discussed.

JONAH

KEY VERSES

Jonah set out on the first day of his walk in the city and proclaimed, "In forty days Nineveh will be demolished!" Then the people of Nineveh believed God. They proclaimed a fast and dressed in sackcloth—from the greatest of them to the least.

— Jonah 3:4-5

BASIC FACTS

1. A reluctant, eighth-century BC Israelite prophet of the Lord to the Assyrian city of Nineveh.

2. Hebrew name *Jonah* means "dove."

3. Son of Amittai from Gath-hepher, a town located west of the Sea of Galilee, two miles north of Nazareth.

4. Survived being thrown overboard in a raging Mediterranean storm when a great fish swallowed and later regurgitated him on shore.

5. His age and circumstances of death are unknown.

TIMELINE

800–750 BC

- Uzziah reigns in Judah 794–740
- 1st Olympic Games held in Greece 776
- Jonah's prophetic ministry 770
- 1st documented solar eclipse in Assyria 763

750–700 BC

- Isaiah's prophetic ministry 742–700
- Tiglath-pileser III rules in Assyria 745–727
- Syro-Ephraimite war against Judah 735
- Northern Kingdom conquered by Assyria 722
- Hezekiah rules in Judah 715–686
- Sennacherib (Assyria) invades Judah 701

KNOWN FOR

1. Jonah went the opposite direction when God called him to prophesy judgment in the Assyrian city of Nineveh. He went to the coastal city of Joppa and there boarded a ship sailing west to Tarshish (Jonah 1:1-4).

2. When God sent a raging storm against the ship Jonah was in, the disobedient prophet was thrown overboard and swallowed by a great fish. Jonah spent three days and nights in the fish before being regurgitated onto dry land (Jonah 1:4–2:10).

3. Jonah obeyed God's second commission to prophesy in Nineveh. His message about the city's impending destruction was met with repentance by both king and citizens (Jonah 3).

4. Jonah became angry when God spared Nineveh as a result of the people's repentance. God then had to teach His prophet a lesson in compassionate mercy through a shade plant (Jonah 4).

5. Jonah's three days and nights in the fish later became a prophetic sign about Jesus' time in the grave before His resurrection (Matt. 12:38-41).

700–600 BC

- Sennacherib destroys city of Babylon 689
- His son, Esarhaddon, rebuilds Babylon 676
- Josiah reigns in Judah 640–609
- Josiah enacts reforms; finds the law 631–622
- Jeremiah's prophetic ministry 627–585
- Assyrian Empire ends with fall of Nineveh 612
- Daniel and friends taken to Babylon 605

600–500 BC

- Nebuchadnezzar takes Jehoiachin captive 597
- Ezekiel's prophetic ministry 593–570
- Jerusalem destroyed; people captured 586
- Temple of Solomon looted and burned 586
- Cyrus of Persia takes Babylon 539
- Edict of Cyrus allows Jews to return 539
- Second temple completed 515

Jonah: A Prophet for His Time

By Robert C. Dunston

Jonah was the son of Amittai from Gath-hepher (see 2 Kings 14:25), which was located about three miles northeast of Nazareth, in the Northern Kingdom of Israel. Jonah's ministry likely occurred in the first half of the eighth century BC. God called Jonah to go to the city of Nineveh. Dating back to approximately 4500 BC, Nineveh, although not the capital, was one of the larger and more important cities of Assyria, the dominant world power of the day. Nineveh's ruler and citizenry would have represented the entire nation's glory, power, dreams, and sin. No Israelite would have wanted to set foot in Nineveh. Perhaps Jonah's reluctance reflected his fear of how the Assyrians, who had no knowledge of God, would respond to his preaching.

Separate from Jonah's prophetic ministry in Nineveh, God gave Jonah a positive message to preach to Israel's King Jeroboam II (ruled 793–753 BC). God would extend Israel's northern border to Lebohamath, the northernmost border during Solomon's reign (see 14:25-26).

Jeroboam II was an evil king; he continued the sins of Jeroboam I, the first king of the Northern Kingdom (see v. 24). Despite his sinfulness, Jeroboam II lived in a fortunate time. Due to the internal weaknesses in the kingdom of Assyria, both Israel and Judah enjoyed almost forty years of independence and prosperity.

Jeroboam II took advantage of Assyria's weakness and exercised authority over Israel's neighbors in the north, Damascus and Hamath (see v. 28), and possibly the Moabites and Ammonites in the southern Transjordan. Both Israel and Judah profited financially by controlling major trade routes through their territories, and the Red Sea may have again become a lucrative channel for foreign trade. Various industries flourished, and many people believed this prosperity was a sign of God's pleasure and blessing upon Israel.

Under the external signs of peace and prosperity, Israel, however, was suffering from sin and decay. The prosperity the wealthy enjoyed did not reach the poor. Through drought, crop failures, and taxation, small farmers struggled to sustain themselves and their families. Many lost ancestral lands and became hired servants to the wealthy, who enlarged their holdings and increased their wealth through the misfortunes of the poor.

Robert C. Dunston, "Jonah: A Prophet for His Time." *Biblical Illustrator*, Summer 2015.

While worshipers filled the temple in Jerusalem and the religious shrines in Israel, the people were merely going through the required rituals, believing this was all God wanted (see Amos 4:4-5; 5:21-23). The people, priests, and prophets had no true knowledge of God and what He desired (see Hos. 4:1-6). The people were worshiping the Lord and false gods (see vv. 12-14).

The peace and prosperity did not last. Assyria experienced a resurgence under Tiglath-pileser III (744–727 BC). In 734 BC, Assyria reduced the size of the kingdom of Israel to the immediate territory surrounding the capital of Samaria. The next Assyrian ruler, Shalmaneser V (726–722 BC) besieged Samaria for three years; the Northern Kingdom fell and Shalmaneser's successor Sargon II (722–705 BC) deported most of the inhabitants of Samaria to other parts of the Assyrian Empire.

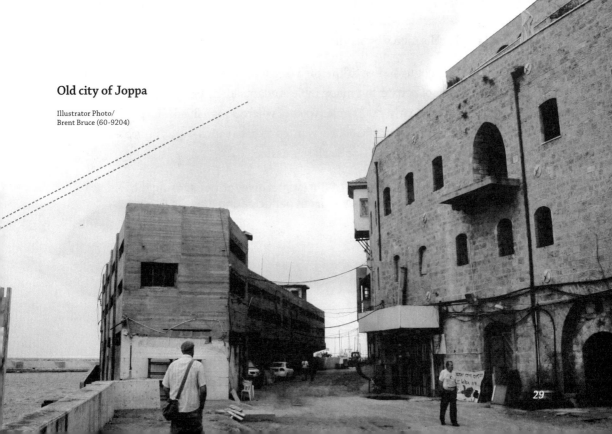

Old city of Joppa

Illustrator Photo/
Brent Bruce (60-9204)

Read Jonah 1:1-17.

The Book of Jonah's opening verses reveal why Bible students sometimes refer to Jonah as "the reluctant prophet." When the Lord called him to go to the city of Nineveh and preach against that people's wickedness, Jonah fled in the opposite direction.

Exactly how Jonah received the word of the Lord isn't explained. We know from other Bible texts that the Lord used various means to communicate to His prophets, including visions (see Isa. 2:1), everyday events (see Jer. 18:1-4), and even a soft, whispering voice (see 1 Kings 19:12-13). However Jonah received the divine message, a significant truth of the opening verse of the book is that our Infinite Creator, the Sovereign Lord, chooses to interact directly and clearly with His people about His purposes.

Equally amazing is the reality that God calls His people to participate with Him in fulfilling those purposes. For Jonah, that call came in specific and urgent terms. The command in verse 2 to "Get up!" meant that the Lord wanted him to act immediately. The need was urgent. People's destinies were at stake.

Jonah's mission was not only urgent, but also specific. The Lord wanted him to travel to Nineveh. There he was to preach against the great wickedness of the people in that city. Their wickedness was repugnant to the Lord, and He planned to judge them. Yet He also would display His mercy by sending His prophet to warn them.

Jonah immediately got up to flee to Tarshish (see v. 3). The exact location of ancient Tarshish is a matter of debate, but many Bible students identify it with an area located on the coast of Spain, nearly 2,000 miles west of where Jonah lived. The point is clear: Jonah acted in rebellion against God. He wanted to get as far away as possible from the Lord's presence and, thus, from God's call to mission.

What are some reasons you've heard Christians give for not sharing the gospel with others? What hinders you from participating more in God's worldwide gospel mission?

Jonah settled in for the long voyage by going to sleep in the ship's lower compartment (see v. 5). He had no clue what was happening around him. The Lord decided to make the prophet's rebellious journey a teachable moment. He hurled a violent wind on the sea, producing such a terrible storm that the ship was in danger of breaking apart.

Has the Lord ever used life events to get your attention about following Him completely? If so, what was the event, and how did you respond?

After Jonah was exposed as the one responsible for God's sending the storm (see v. 7), the sailors began to interrogate him. The prophet openly testified that he worshiped the God who created everything, including the land and water (see v. 9). Jonah's profession revealed his understanding and affirmation of God's sovereignty, although his actions up to this point contradicted his beliefs.

Upon hearing Jonah's words, the sailors became even more afraid, exclaiming, "What is this you have done?" (v. 10.) Even unbelievers could see the foolishness of Jonah's disobedient actions. The prophet's instruction for the sailors to throw him into the sea is striking! Jonah was still thinking and acting in rebellion against the Lord. He had admitted his guilt to the ship's crew, but the text gives no evidence that he'd repented of his sins to the Lord. He just wanted to escape.

The Bible is God's story of redeeming love for sinful people. That truth should spur us to serve God without reservation. Yet, like Jonah, we're sometimes tempted to opt out, to run in the opposite direction from God's call to mission. What will it take for us to follow our Lord Jesus Christ obediently?

What is something you think God may be asking you to do right now? What will it mean for you to go where God leads?

Read Jonah 3:1-10.

Jonah's life story teaches us that the Lord is a God of second chances. If we falter in our faith or service, He will pursue us to get us back on the track of faithfulness.

Expelled from the belly of the fish onto dry land, the rebellious prophet found himself again compelled by the word of the Lord. The urgent mission hadn't changed. Jonah's instructions were essentially the same as the first time, expressed in three imperatives: "Get up! Go to . . . Nineveh . . . preach the message that I tell you" (Jonah 3:1-2). The Lord gave Jonah another opportunity to participate in His worldwide mission.

When has God given you a second chance? How did you respond to your second chance?

This time when God said, "Get up and go!" Jonah got up and went. He acted in obedience to the Lord's command. He decided that obedience was better than the belly of a fish.

The city of Nineveh was an extremely large city, even by ancient standards. It served as one of the prominent capital cities of the Assyrian Empire. It took Jonah three days to reach all parts of this large, populous city with God's message (see v. 3).

On the first day of Jonah's visit to Nineveh, he declared that the city would be demolished in forty days (see v. 4). Perhaps this was a summary of a lengthier, more detailed message. Regardless, this was the bottom line of an urgent warning from God. If there was a possibility of mercy and forgiveness for the Ninevites through repentance, Jonah didn't mention it at this time.

We as believers need to be reminded that the need is urgent for all people to hear the gospel of Jesus Christ and have an opportunity to respond. Every person apart from Christ is lost and under threat of God's eternal judgment. May we respond to that urgent need with Christlike compassion, seeking ways to tell all people about God's provision of forgiveness and eternal life.

The people's reaction to Jonah's blunt message was astounding. Three verbs in verse 5 describe their response. First, they believed in God. Although they were wicked and idolatrous, the people of Nineveh turned in their belief to the God whom Jonah served. Second, they proclaimed a fast as a sign of repentance from their evil behavior. Third, they all dressed in sackcloth as a further sign of grief over their plight.

Jonah must have been shocked when genuine repentance began to ripple through Nineveh. Across barriers of language, culture, and hatred, God's Word made the difference. Led by their king, the Ninevites humbled themselves before God and went to great lengths to express their plea for God's mercy (see vv. 6-9). The door of God's heart swung gently open. The relentless Pursuer saw the Ninevites' genuine acts of repentance and relented from the disaster He had threatened (see v. 10). Jonah's preaching had accomplished the Lord's intended purpose. We know the change was real because Jesus referred to the repentance of the Ninevites as genuine (see Luke 11:32).

What is surprising about the Ninevites' response to Jonah's message? When have you been surprised by a conversion story?

What people groups or individuals do we sometimes assume won't be receptive to the message of Christ today? What factors would convince you otherwise?

We should never assume that someone will reject the gospel. God has called us to be sensitive to the needs around us and faithful in sharing. God will accept anyone who comes to Him humbly and with repentance. The whole reason God sent His Son was to bring people—all people—back to Him. We have a responsibility to share because we never know how He intends to fulfill His plan through us.

Read Jonah 4:1-11.

Technically, Jonah had obeyed God. After being spit out of the belly of a fish, he went to Nineveh and spoke God's message there. He did as God asked, but his heart wasn't in it. After the Ninevites repented and were saved, Jonah went outside the city to pout.

Jonah became greatly displeased and furious when he learned the Lord wasn't going to destroy Nineveh. His excuse for initially running away to Tarshish boiled to the surface again. In essence Jonah argued, "God, I knew you'd get me over to Nineveh to prophesy doom; then You'd change Your mind at the smallest hint of repentance" (see v. 2). What Jonah exposed in his prayer, however, was his deep misunderstanding of God's ultimate purpose to include all nations in His redemptive plan.

How easy is it to criticize Jonah's lack of compassion? Why should we think twice before doing so?

Jonah prayed for the Lord to take His life, saying, "It is better for me to die than to live" (v. 3). Perhaps Jonah felt that he was now a discredited prophet and the Lord's compassion for sinners was to blame for his misery. After all, what he had predicted would happen to Nineveh did not happen.

God answered Jonah's prayer with a simple rhetorical question: "Is it right for you to be angry?" (v. 4). God's loving approach to Jonah encouraged him to pause and reflect. The prophet's anger was inappropriate, and God wanted to help Jonah understand His compassion for all people, not just for the people of Israel.

After being questioned by God, Jonah headed east, stopping outside the city. Here the Lord "appointed a plant . . . to provide shade" for Jonah (v. 6) The plant's shade helped ease Jonah's discomfort. The next day God appointed a worm to eat the plant, removing Jonah's shade. The large leaves that had provided shade wilted to nothing. But just to be sure Jonah didn't miss the point, the Lord appointed a scorching east wind. Besides filling the air with dust and sand, the desert wind probably blew away

Jonah's crude shelter. Now there was nothing to shield the prophet from the intense heat and sunlight. Jonah nearly passed out and in his misery declared again that he wanted to die (see vv. 7-8).

God again spoke to Jonah, asking the prophet if it was right for him to be angry about the plant (see v. 9). Though Jonah attempted to justify his anger, God used the situation to teach His prophet a lesson about compassion. If Jonah could care for a mere plant, should God not care about the eternity of 120,000 people?

What are some of the "plants" you embrace in your life? How might they keep you from embracing the needs of those who don't know Christ?

If we are to genuinely pursue God's will, we must not pursue self-seeking desires. God and His interests should be the top priority in our lives, and obedience to Him should guide all our actions.

Notice that the Book of Jonah ends with a question mark (see v. 11). We're left without knowing whether the prophet changed his attitude and behavior.

How does the open-ended conclusion to the Book of Jonah impact how you read the book?

In leaving the book open-ended, the Lord can use it today to probe our attitudes about divine grace and compassion for the lost peoples of the world. Millions of people have never heard the gospel of Jesus Christ. Christ's commission propels us as believers to make disciples of all nations.

ISAIAH

The Prophet Who Predicted Jesus

INTRODUCTION

Isaiah lived in troubled and tumultuous times. Three hundred years before the prophet ministered, David had drawn the tribes together, subdued surrounding nations, and carved out a secure Israelite state. The luster of David's golden age started to fade during his son Solomon's reign. Following Solomon's death, the nation divided into the Northern Kingdom of Israel and the Southern Kingdom of Judah.

At the beginning of the eighth century BC, both Israel and Judah were prosperous and secure. But by the time Isaiah lived and ministered in the last half of the eighth century, the neighboring nation of Assyria had begun a policy of expansion and conquest. This would result in the destruction of Israel and leave Judah vulnerable and paying tribute to the Assyrians.

Think of the questions the people of Judah must have had. Was their nation in crisis because their God was weaker than the Assyrian gods? Is military force the determining factor in a nation's security? What did their future hold? Who could speak for God in such a time?

The answers to such questions came at a pivotal moment in Judah's history—when the good king Uzziah died. That was the year Isaiah received a call to be the Lord's prophet. For more than four decades Isaiah faithfully shared God's messages to Judah—both the difficult message of judgment and the comforting message of hope.

When have you been faced with speaking a difficult message to someone? How about delivering a comforting message of hope?

In what ways did you experience the Lord preparing you for the conversations you needed to have?

Watch the video teaching for Session 3 to discover "The World of Isaiah," then continue the group discussion.

FOCUS ATTENTION

What factors determine whether we view serving God as a privilege or a burden?

EXPLORE THE TEXT

As a group, read Isaiah 6:1-4.

These verses focus on the revelation of God's holiness to Isaiah. What's significant about the timing of Isaiah's vision? Why do you think God chose this particular time to reveal Himself to Isaiah?

What are some ways God reveals His glory to people today?

As a group, read Isaiah 6:5-7.

Describe the connection between how one sees God and how one responds to God. Why did Isaiah's vision shift from focusing on God's glory to realizing his own unworthiness in verse 5?

What would have become of Isaiah if the story had ended with verse 5? Why do we often end our stories with feelings of inadequacy?

As a group, read Isaiah 6:8-10.

Why did God pose a request for someone to send and not a command to go?

Why would God send a messenger to people who weren't going to listen?

APPLY THE TEXT

The prophet Isaiah came face to face with the glory of God, and his life was forever changed. When we are confronted with God's holy nature, the only acceptable response is worship and surrender to His will. No excuse for not serving God will carry weight in the light of His holy and glorious nature.

How does your understanding of God's holiness compare to Isaiah's experience?

What effect should God's holy character have on the choices you make this week?

How might unconfessed sin keep us from seeing and delighting in God's glory? What do you need to confess and repent of today following Isaiah's example?

Close your group time in prayer, reflecting on what you have discussed.

ISAIAH

KEY VERSE

Then I heard the voice of the Lord asking: Who should I send? Who will go for us? I said: Here I am. Send me.

— Isaiah 6:8

BASIC FACTS

1. Long-serving eighth-century BC Israelite prophet during the reigns of four kings in Judah.

2. Hebrew name *Isaiah*—like *Joshua, Hosea,* and the Greek name *Jesus*—means "Yahweh (the Lord) saves" or "Yahweh is salvation."

3. Son of Amoz, an otherwise unknown Israelite but whom Jewish rabbinic tradition suggests was related to the royal lineage of King David.

4. Married, but wife's name unknown; two sons: Shear-jashub (meaning "a remnant will return") and Maher-shalal-hash-baz (meaning "speeding to the plunder; hastening to the spoils").

5. Age at death unknown in Scripture; Jewish rabbinic tradition suggests a martyr's death during the reign of Hezekiah's son, Manasseh.

TIMELINE

800–750 BC

- Uzziah reigns in Judah 794–740
- First Olympic Games held in Greece 776
- Jonah's prophetic ministry 770
- First documented solar eclipse in Assyria 763

750–700 BC

- Isaiah's prophetic ministry 742–700
- Tiglath-pileser III rules in Assyria 745–727
- Syro-Ephraimite war against Judah 735
- Northern Kingdom conquered by Assyria 722
- Hezekiah rules in Judah 715–686
- Sennacherib (Assyria) invades Judah 701

KNOWN FOR

1. God called Isaiah to be a prophet in a vision of the Lord on His heavenly throne that likely took place in the temple soon after the death of Uzziah, the second longest reigning king of Judah—52 years (Isa. 6).

2. Isaiah's literary skills were exquisite and effective. He was a master of both poetry and narrative, using prophetic oracles, parables, historical reports, prayers, songs, and letters to reveal what God was doing (and would do) from his own time in eighth century BC to the end times.

3. The Book of Isaiah is quoted more in the New Testament concerning the Messiah than any Old Testament book.

4. Isaiah challenged King Hezekiah of Judah to trust in the Lord for deliverance from the Assyrian threat of destruction by Sennacherib in 701 BC (2 Kings 19:1-7). The prophet later delivered a message to Hezekiah that the king would soon die, only to be sent back to the king later with a message that God was giving Hezekiah fifteen more years to live (2 Kings 20:1-11).

5. Isaiah wrote the four so-called "Servant Songs" as part of his messianic prophecies (Isa. 42:1-4; 49:1-6; 50:4-7; 52:13–53:12).

700–600 BC

- Sennacherib destroys city of Babylon 689
- His son, Esarhaddon, rebuilds Babylon 676
- Josiah reigns in Judah 640–609
- Josiah enacts reforms; finds the law 631–622
- Jeremiah's prophetic ministry 627–585
- Assyrian Empire ends with fall of Nineveh 612
- Daniel and friends taken to Babylon 605

600–500 BC

- Nebuchadnezzar takes Jehoiachin captive 597
- Ezekiel's prophetic ministry 593–570
- Jerusalem destroyed; people captured 586
- Temple of Solomon looted and burned 586
- Cyrus of Persia takes Babylon 539
- Edict of Cyrus allows Jews to return 539
- Second temple completed 515

Isaiah's Messianic Prophecies

By Stephen R. Miller

The centerpiece of both Isaiah's message and God's plan for the redemption of the human race was the Messiah. No prophet gives a more complete picture of the Messiah's persona and work than the prophet Isaiah. These Old Testament prophecies of the Messiah's first coming were perfectly fulfilled in the life and ministry of Jesus of Nazareth.

Messianic Prophecies

Messiah as King—Isaiah depicted the Messiah most frequently as King. In Isaiah 4:2-6, Messiah's royal ancestry ("the Branch" from David's line; compare Isa. 11:1; Jer. 23:5; 33:15) and glorious future reign are in view. In Isaiah 7:1-16, the prophet predicted King Messiah's miraculous birth—to a virgin! Matthew positively identified this child as Jesus, the son of the virgin Mary (Matt. 1:20-23). Messiah will be history's most amazing King (Isa. 9:1-7). The "son" of the virgin will be the "Mighty God" (an epithet for Yahweh Himself; 10:21; Jer. 32:18) and the "Eternal Father" (the eternal and therefore uncreated source of all creation). His reign will never end. Isaiah described the peace and safety of Messiah's universal reign in terms of a return to garden of Eden conditions (see Isa. 11:1-16, cf. 65:25). The loving and just reign of our King is stressed in Isaiah 16:5.

Messiah as Servant (Priest)—Four passages in Isaiah are known as "Servant Songs" (see 42:1-9; 49:1-13; 50:4-11; 52:13–53:12). These passages depict the coming Messiah as the Lord's faithful "Servant." He is obedient to the Father's will and fulfills His priestly work of redemption.

The first Servant Song (see 42:1-9; Jesus Christ, according to Matt. 12:15-21) emphasizes the Messiah's character. Both the first and second Servant Songs assert the inevitable success of His mission as a spiritual "light to the nations" (Isa. 42:6; 49:6). Though "despised" at His first advent, Christ will someday receive the honor He deserves (see 49:7; compare Phil. 2:10-11). Isaiah predicted Christ's mockery and torture in the third Servant Song (see Isa. 50:4-11; compare Matt. 26:67; 27:26,30-31, 39-44). Yet with God's help, the Servant would fulfill His mission and overcome all opposition (Isa. 50:7-9). The third Song concludes with a frightening warning to trust in the true spiritual light (Messiah) or face "torment" (vv. 10-11).

Prophecy   fulfillment

Google - Chart of Old Testements Prophecies fulfilled by Jesus

The Servant of Isaiah's fourth Servant Song is none other than Jesus of Nazareth (compare Acts 8:30-35). Here Isaiah described the Messiah's atonement for our sin at Calvary (especially Isa. 53:4-6,8,11-12). Though not labeled a servant song, Isaiah 55:3-5 depicts the Servant offering salvation (made possible by His atonement) to all nations.

Living with Anticipation

The fulfillment of these messianic prophecies would have been centuries in the future for Isaiah's original audience. Regardless of the exact time of fulfillment, these promises assured Isaiah that someday God would raise up a Savior for sin and a righteous Ruler who would bring world peace, security, and freedom from tyrants.

Stephen R. Miller, "Isaiah's Messianic Prophecies," *Biblical Illustrator,* Spring 2006.

Read Isaiah 1:1-20.

Much of what we know about Isaiah the prophet is found in the first verse of the book that bears his name. He was the son of Amoz, and his ministry spanned four kings of Judah (Uzziah, Jotham, Ahaz, and Hezekiah). According to Jewish tradition, Isaiah's father, Amoz, was the brother of Amaziah, an earlier king of Judah. If this is correct, then Isaiah and King Uzziah were cousins. This may help explain Isaiah's connections with people in high offices and his ready access to Judah's kings (see 2 Kings 19:1-2,20; 20:1, 2 Chron. 32:20).

Isaiah was the earliest of the God-called major prophets; the others were Jeremiah, Ezekiel, and Daniel. (The major prophets are called major because of the length of their books.) Many Bible readers consider Isaiah the most poetic of all the prophets in his use of written and spoken imagery about God judging the nation of Judah. God inspired Isaiah to speak words that would shake the people out of their rebellion and complacency toward Him.

Was there a time in your life when studying and hearing God's Word seemed meaningless? If so, what changed your mind, or do you still tend to be complacent toward His Word?

As you read Isaiah 1:2-4, notice that the setting could be a courtroom scene with God as prosecutor and judge. As the trial began, God called the heavens and the earth as witnesses to hear the charges against Judah. The people rebelled against God—like rebellious teenagers.

List some areas where you see people rebelling against God in our culture today. Now list at least two areas where you have rebelled against God.

God called the people of Judah His "children" (v. 2). Judah was able to call God their Father because of His conscious, continuous, loving commitment to them. He had chosen them, redeemed them through the exodus from Egypt, led and cared for them in the wilderness, and brought them into Canaan. God's dedication to His children made Judah's rebellion more inexplicable. Judah turned against its loving, nurturing Father and refused to be and do what God intended.

When we ignore God and choose our own path through life, we face the consequences of our self-centered decisions and the righteous anger of God who desires us to follow Him. Judah already had suffered for its sin. Isaiah's words in verses 5-9 probably reflect earlier destruction in Judah by the Assyrians. God was using the Assyrians to punish His people for their sin. Judah, however, did not understand that its present difficulty was punishment by God meant to cause them to return to Him.

The nation's rebellion against God had also affected its worship. Isaiah told them that God was not satisfied with the religious practices of His people (vv. 11-15). Though they loved their traditional feasts, ceremonies, and sacrifices, their religious rituals were empty of true praise and sincere worship.

What could you do to make your worship experiences more meaningful?

God's remedy for His people involved repentance (v. 16). If they would turn away from their sins and spiritual complacency, He would cleanse them. He also expected them to pursue justice and promote the interests of the vulnerable—the fatherless and the widow (v. 17).

Isaiah's message presented two options to the people (vv. 18-20). One was to repent and obey. A remarkable transformation would then result. The second option was continued rebellion, a course of action that would end with their destruction. The choice was theirs.

Read Isaiah 6:1-13.

For fifty years King Uzziah had ruled the Southern Kingdom of Judah. An able administrator and effective military leader, this king brought a period of prosperity and stability to his nation. He died in 740 BC with the Assyrian threat looming over his land. Uzziah's death signaled a national crisis and made many in Judah and Jerusalem feel hopeless.

Isaiah might have felt discouraged also. God chose this moment, however, to give the prophet a vision of Himself. In this exalted moment, the Lord called Isaiah to serve Him, commissioning him as His messenger to the people of Judah.

In the vision recorded in chapter 6, Isaiah saw the Lord "seated on a high and lofty throne" (v. 1). *Sitting on the throne* emphasizes the Lord as the true King of Judah and *being in the temple* emphasizes His holiness. Judah lost its earthly king, Uzziah, but the true and eternal King is always on His throne.

Isaiah saw seraphim standing above the Lord (v. 2). The word *seraphim* means "the burning ones" or "the fiery ones." Seraphim appear in the Bible only in Isaiah's vision. The key characteristic of God lauded by these angels was His holiness. "Holy" is repeated three times for emphasis. *Holiness* describes the presence of complete perfection and the absence of imperfection.

When have you been guilty of making God too small in your thoughts? What measures could you take to guard against minimizing God in your thinking?

Isaiah's response to these heavenly sights and sounds was an overpowering recognition of sin. He looked at the Lord and then looked at himself, and his conclusion was, "I am ruined" (v. 5). He expressed a deep despair concerning his sin and knew there was nothing he could do. If the Lord did not provide a remedy, no remedy could be found.

How might unconfessed sin keep us from seeing and delighting in God's glory? Following Isaiah's example, what do you need to confess and repent of today?

Isaiah also declared himself "a man of unclean lips" (v. 5). In response to his confession, the Lord sent one of the seraphim who took a glowing coal from the altar, approached Isaiah with it in his hand, and touched the prophet's lips (vv. 6-7). The touching of Isaiah's lips symbolized the removal of all his sin; his sin was atoned for. *Atonement* refers to the process of removing the guilt and barriers created by sin. The concept of atonement implies the necessity of payment and a substitute to redeem the sinner. Jesus provided our atonement through His death and resurrection.

After removing the prophet's sin, the Lord issued a call to service. He sought a volunteer to go. Though the Lord was surrounded by angelic messengers (the seraphim), He desired a human messenger to confront the sinful nation. Isaiah, after he was cleansed from his sin, responded, "Send me."

Isaiah's heartfelt response was immediate and to the point, telling God he was ready to go. He didn't know yet where he would go or what he would do. Still, he volunteered to serve. He surrendered himself completely for the Lord's service.

How would you evaluate your willingness to serve God whenever, wherever, and however? What barriers keep you from serving God?

Immediately after Isaiah's willing response, God prepared him for what would be a difficult ministry (vv. 9-10). God did not leave Isaiah hopeless; He pointed to a remnant who would return to the Lord (v. 13). Judgment would fall upon the sinful people of Judah because of God's justice. But because of the Lord's mercy and grace, He would never completely eradicate His promise of salvation that would ultimately come through the person and work of Jesus Christ.

Read Isaiah 53:1-12.

While Isaiah's message in chapters 1–39 focused primarily on God's judgment of His people and the nations, the prophet's message in the remaining chapters was about hope. The last part of his book (chapters 40–66) was addressed to later generations and would comfort God's people returning to their land from Babylonian exile.

Judah would fully experience the Lord's punishment of destruction and domination by a foreign power. But that would not be the end of their story. God would work in unexpected ways through unexpected people to deal with their root problem of sin.

In chapter 53, Isaiah explained God's plan to bring salvation to His people and to all nations through the future coming of the Messiah. This Servant would suffer, but through His suffering He would bear the punishment for all human sin and provide forgiveness for all (see 52:13–53:12). This Servant of whom Isaiah spoke is Jesus. The New Testament applies Isaiah 53 to Jesus in Matthew 27:38,57-60; Acts 8:32-34; and 1 Peter 2:22-23.

Isaiah described the Suffering Servant as "a root out of dry ground" (Isa. 53:2), meaning the Messiah would come in an unexpected time and way. He would not fit the stereotype of a savior for His people. As we know, Jesus grew up in relative obscurity in the town of Nazareth. Nazareth did not possess a good reputation, possibly because of a lack of culture and moral laxity. When Nathanael heard that Jesus came from Nazareth, he was surprised (see John 1:45-46).

Isaiah described how people would view the Servant (v. 3). Many would consider Him contemptible and disgusting and, consequently, reject Him. Pain and suffering were distinctive characteristics of His life. "Sickness" refers to the consequences of sin as made clear in verse 4. Therefore, the Servant would know what it is like to live in a fallen world. People would treat Him as if He were worthless.

Many people today think of Jesus as having no significance or value for them. In what ways have you been guilty of not valuing Him or underestimating His significance?

What would be the purpose of the Servant's suffering? In verses 4-6, Isaiah explained the Servant would suffer on behalf of others—"because of our rebellion." Though not suffering for His own sins, the Servant would suffer silently and willingly (v. 7).

Verse 9 speaks of the Servant's burial. His executioners would dishonor Him by treating Him like a criminal. Nevertheless, the Servant would be given an honorable burial after His dishonorable death, because He was without sin.

That God was "pleased to crush" the Servant (see Isa. 53:10) sounds harsh, but Isaiah explained God's pleasure by the fact that the Servant's suffering would justify many (v. 11). What seemed harsh, turned out to be gracious. God sent His Son because there was no other way for us to be forgiven and have fellowship with Him. The death of Jesus was a restitution offering, an offering for sin. Jesus paid the price for sin and releases believers from the debt incurred by sin.

Jesus perfectly fulfilled Isaiah's portrait of the Suffering Servant. By His suffering, humiliation, and death, Jesus provided forgiveness and new life. Though beaten and killed, He was triumphant. His suffering gave way to His exaltation (see Isa. 53:12). Jesus' suffering culminated in the crucifixion, but it gave way to the resurrection. Those who put their faith in Him receive the free gift of eternal life.

How does this passage reassure you of God's forgiveness and love?

How would you use Isaiah 53 to explain the purpose and mission of Jesus Christ to someone who had never heard of Him?

JEREMIAH

The Weeping Prophet

INTRODUCTION

One of the most pivotal prophets in Israel's history began as a young, unassuming character. He doubted his ability to carry out the Lord's assignment, even after God Himself spoke the marching orders directly into his life. Jeremiah had to learn that God's people can accomplish any assignment the Lord gives to the extent they trust in His presence and power along the way.

Jeremiah is sometimes called "the weeping prophet" because of his personal anguish over Judah's sin and their impending captivity. He seemed to live in constant friction with the authorities and the people themselves. Jeremiah spoke hard messages of judgment. Sometimes he didn't want to speak the word he was called to speak. He was honest about his unhappiness with the situation and sometimes expressed his frustration to God.

Through it all, Jeremiah would remain faithful to God's call. His success ultimately lay in being faithful to God's call and trusting God as he boldly delivered the Lord's message.

When have you been frustrated with God for something He called you to do? What caused your frustration?

How did you deal with the situation?

Watch the video teaching for Session 4 to discover "The World of Jeremiah," then continue the group discussion.

GROUP DISCUSSION

FOCUS ATTENTION

What is one of the most difficult assignments you've had in your professional or personal life? How did you find the ability to deal with that assignment?

EXPLORE THE TEXT

As a group, read Jeremiah 1:4-6.

How did Jeremiah recognize God's call to a specific ministry?

What can we learn about the nature of God's calling from Jeremiah?

As a group, read Jeremiah 1:7-10.

How did God react to Jeremiah's doubts and excuses? What provisions did God make for Jeremiah despite his youth?

What excuses do we make today for not serving the Lord? How does God respond to these excuses?

What are some specific ways God provides His people today with power to accomplish the tasks to which He calls them?

As a group, read Jeremiah 1:11-16.

What object lessons did God use to reassure Jeremiah? How did these lessons encourage Jeremiah that the Lord would fulfill His promise to bring judgment (which was the content of Jeremiah's message)?

As a group, read Jeremiah 1:17-19.

What would make God's message a difficult one for Jeremiah to deliver?

What are some practical ways you can be prepared for confronting opposition as you stand for truth?

APPLY THE TEXT

Jeremiah's success and victory lay in faithfully delivering the Lord's message. In the same way, the Lord is the One who assures our success. God desires that we rely on and obey Him regardless of our situation. We can trust God with our calling because He knows the end of the story.

What are some of the obstacles that get in the way of believers living out their calling?

What reassurances from the life of Jeremiah would help you move forward in faith toward what God has called you to do?

Close your group time in prayer, reflecting on what you have discussed.

JEREMIAH

KEY VERSE

I say, "I won't mention him or speak any longer in his name." But his message becomes a fire burning in my heart, shut up in my bones. I become tired of holding it in, and I cannot prevail.

— Jeremiah 20:9

BASIC FACTS

1. Long-serving, faithful prophet of the Lord during the forty years prior to and two years after Jerusalem's destruction by the Babylonians in 586 BC.

2. Name *Jeremiah* means "Yahweh (the Lord) exalts" or "Yahweh is exalted."

3. Son of Hilkiah, a priest of Anathoth, a village located three miles north of Jerusalem.

4. Learned as a youth that his calling even before birth was to be a prophet of the Lord.

5. Remained celibate during his lifetime in obedience to God's instruction.

6. Taken against his will to Egypt after 586 BC, where he probably died a few years later.

TIMELINE

750–700 BC

- Isaiah's prophetic ministry 742–700
- Tiglath-pileser III rules in Assyria 745–727
- Syro-Ephraimite war against Judah 735
- Northern Kingdom conquered by Assyria 722
- Hezekiah rules in Judah 715–686
- Sennacherib (Assyria) invades Judah 701

700–600 BC

- Sennacherib destroys city of Babylon 689
- His son, Esarhaddon, rebuilds Babylon 676
- Josiah reigns in Judah 640–609
- Josiah enacts reforms; finds the law 631–622
- Jeremiah's prophetic ministry 627–585
- Assyrian Empire ends with fall of Nineveh 612
- Daniel and friends taken to Babylon 605

KNOWN FOR

1. Jeremiah was the most self-revealing of the Old Testament prophets. He freely acknowledged his pre-birth destiny to be a prophet (1:5), his lack of self-confidence about that calling (1:6), his anguish over the coming fate of Judah (4:19-21), his questions about the Lord's ways (12:1), his angry prayer for vengeance against his oppressors (15:15), his accusations against the Lord (20:7), and yet his inability to stop proclaiming the Lord's messages (20:9).

2. Jeremiah has been called "the weeping prophet" because he authored numerous laments, including those in the Book of Lamentations.

3. He understood the importance of writing down God's messages as Scripture, doing so in the time of King Jehoiakim and then rewriting it after Jehoiakim destroyed the first scroll (Jer. 36).

4. Although he prophesied accurately that Jerusalem would be destroyed in 586 BC and many Jews would be taken as captives to Babylon, Jeremiah survived the catastrophe and remained in the land of Judah until a group of survivors forced him to go with them as refugees to Egypt (Jer. 40:1-6; 43:1-7).

5. Jeremiah foresaw that the Lord would one day establish a new covenant with His people not based on the law but on grace, faith, and forgiveness (Jer. 31:31-34). The New Testament proclaims that Jesus was the fulfillment of God's promised new covenant (Luke 22:20; 1 Cor. 11:25; Heb. 8:7-12; 9:15-28).

600–500 BC

- Nebuchadnezzar takes Jehoiachin captive 597
- Ezekiel's prophetic ministry 593–570
- Jerusalem destroyed; people captured 586
- Temple of Solomon looted and burned 586
- Cyrus of Persia takes Babylon 539
- Edict of Cyrus allows Jews to return 539
- Second temple completed 515

500–400 BC

- Greeks defeat Persians at Marathon 490
- Esther becomes queen in Persia 479
- Golden age of Greek art 477–431
- Malachi's prophetic ministry 460 (early date)
- Jerusalem's wall rebuilt under Nehemiah 445
- Malachi's prophetic ministry 430 (late date)
- Old Testament biblical record falls silent 400

The Prophet Jeremiah

By Harper Shannon

Jeremiah was born to a priestly family in Anathoth, a small village less than four miles northeast of Jerusalem. His family was cultured and godly. Jeremiah himself later owned property and exerted considerable influence among the princely classes.

Undoubtedly Jeremiah was one of the most colorful of the prophets, and all his prophecies bear the imprint of his unique personality. Jeremiah was warm and affectionate, with deep emotion and heart. Thus, his task of testifying against his own people was difficult, and Jeremiah shrank from the original divine call.

Jeremiah's ministry touched upon the reigns of five kings of Judah: Josiah, Jehoahaz, Jehoiakim, Jehoiachin, and Zedekiah. *Josiah* and Jeremiah were apparently on excellent terms, although Jeremiah no doubt was disillusioned with the superficiality of his reforms and condemned the worshipers who depended upon ritual and externals as a substitute for true religion.

Jehoiakim repudiated his father's reforms and greatly oppressed the people to pay for his own extravagance. Jehoiakim, Jeremiah's deadliest enemy, died just in time to escape the Babylonians' wrath. *Zedekiah* provided Jeremiah no respite, although the king respected Jeremiah and secretly sought his advice. The last sight Zedekiah was allowed to see before he was blinded was the murder of his own sons.

The heart of Jeremiah's message to his own beloved people was that, although sin and rebellion bring sure destruction, God is nevertheless grieved by such rebellion and will inevitably win the victory despite the uncooperativeness of His people. Jeremiah denounced the failings of kings and policies, as well as the hypocrisy of ordinary worshipers. His unswerving emphasis was that national rebellion against divine direction and leadership always leads to national destruction and ruin.

Sin deeply wounds the heart of God—a truth expressed in Jeremiah's regretful and hesitant attitude. But God's weeping over sin does not allow His judgment to be assuaged toward the consistently unrepentant nation. Jeremiah watched his people rushing headlong toward the final calamity, as he faithfully proclaimed the warnings of God out of a heart filled with despair. The root sin in the life of the nation was their

Modern Anathoth, which is a few miles east of Jerusalem, was the hometown of Jeremiah the prophet (Jer. 1:1).

Illustrator Photo/ Bob Schatz (9-19-2)

forgetting God and subsequent rebelling against His ways. Jeremiah saw this clearly and repeatedly warned against it, but was unable to stem the tide of rebellion rushing toward national suicide.

Despite the calamity of the nation, however, God's purposes cannot fail. He will, like the potter with the clay, make the covenant again. Here is Jeremiah's declaration of ultimate divine sovereignty: "He made it again." The branch is appointed. The new covenant one day will be made, when the King-Priest has come. Sin will only temporarily thwart God's will, for eventually He will cancel sin and remake the marred vessel. Thus, Jeremiah's message becomes for all ages one of hope and confidence in the sovereignty and purposefulness of the mighty God.

Harper Shannon, "The Prophet Jeremiah," *Biblical Illustrator*, Fall 1974.

Read Jeremiah 1:4-19.

As a youth, Jeremiah heard God's call to be His prophet. In future experiences, Jeremiah would struggle with his mission. However, he never seemed to question the authenticity of his call. The profound realization that God called him would enable Jeremiah to remain firm when otherwise he was ready to quit. The Lord had prepared Jeremiah for this moment.

The mission of God for Jeremiah must have seemed overwhelming. At first, Jeremiah protested that he was not qualified. He argued that he was too young (v. 6). Jeremiah likely was a teenager. In his view, he lacked the qualifications for such an important mission. Human weakness often is a point in which God reveals His vast strength. For any ministry work to be successful, God must empower it. Too often Christians evaluate opportunities to serve the Lord based solely on their talents rather than reliance on Him.

God bluntly rejected Jeremiah's objection. He promised Jeremiah His ongoing presence and power. Jeremiah's ability to speak publicly or to persuade an audience was irrelevant. People needed to hear a word from the Lord. So God promised to provide the message (v. 7).

In his own power, Jeremiah could not have imagined the dramatic events soon to transpire in his world. Yet he did have a grasp of how his hearers likely would respond to him. The certainty of opposition, combined with the uncertainty of other factors, no doubt was frightening. However, God promised, "I will be with you" (v. 8).

While an individual's personal experiences may constitute God's preparation for an assignment, the ultimate resource for ministry is God's presence. Throughout this entire episode, the Lord repeatedly claimed personal responsibility for Jeremiah's assignment. His presence with the young prophet would be sufficient for any situation.

The Lord also provided Jeremiah with His power. The symbolic gesture of touching the mouth (v. 9) signified that Jeremiah was commissioned as a prophet. God declared that He had filled the prophet's mouth with His words, enabling Jeremiah to speak the Lord's message precisely.

Two visions confirmed Jeremiah's mission. In the first one, God showed the prophet a branch of an almond tree, one of the first trees to blossom in the spring (v. 11).

Just as the almond tree blossoms early in Israel's springtime and signifies the coming of a fruitful season, God told Jeremiah that He would soon cause him to "blossom" with fruitful words from God.

What are some ways the Lord reassures you about your calling to service?

In the second vision, Jeremiah saw a boiling pot tilted toward the south, spilling its contents of disaster from the north (vv. 13-15). This was the direction from which foreign armies would come against Israel and Judah. God confirmed that His judgment would pour upon the nation of Judah. The reason for such a severe judgment was Judah's burning incense to other gods (v. 16).

The Lord issued a challenge to Jeremiah (vv. 17-19). The prophet was to speak every word God told him. His hearers would not like what they heard, but he must not waver. To succeed, Jeremiah needed to revere God more than he feared what his hearers might do. Though there would be strong opposition to Jeremiah's message, kings, officials, and priests would not prevail over God's prophet (v. 19).

God measures success not by how others respond to us, but by how faithful and obedient we are in carrying out what He assigns to us. Jeremiah's success lay in faithfully delivering the Lord's message and standing firm in the face of opposition. We too can be confident in our service to the Lord by obeying and depending on Him.

How do you depend on the Lord's resources in your service to Him?

Read Jeremiah 15:10-21.

Jeremiah was a real human being who experienced emotional highs and lows. At times, he struggled with the calling God placed on him, even expressing his complaints to God. These complaints to God are part of what has been called "The Confessions of Jeremiah." Jeremiah 15 records one of those complaints, and God's response.

Jeremiah had faithfully preached God's message that false worship and sinful lifestyles would result in God's impending judgment. Babylon would conquer and destroy everything the people of Judah cherished. In the light of God's inevitable judgment, Jeremiah was left with a sense of defeat. He was filled with bitterness and hopelessness.

Describe a time when you felt hopeless or defeated. How did God respond?

The prophet made a startling confession: he wished he had never been born (v. 10). He wished he could no longer feel pain. It is important to note that even in his lowest times, Jeremiah never talked of ending his own life. Instead he confronted his dilemma by taking it directly to God.

Jeremiah once found God's words delightful (v. 16). Now he lamented that delivering God's message had caused so much strife for his people. He forgot that those words were not his to begin with. God's Word to His children sometimes causes pain. Experiencing the sting of rebuke tells us we have transgressed God's law.

When has God's Word been painful for you to read or understand? How did you resolve the conflict you experienced?

Jeremiah felt he had legitimate grounds for his complaint. His despair, however, had blinded him to reality. God never suggested that Jeremiah would not have opposition. He never promised Jeremiah that his service would be without heartache or opposition. Neither has the Lord made that promise to us.

The lows Jeremiah experienced included loneliness (v. 17), anger (v. 17) and unending pain (v. 18). His lows reached the point of spiritual doubt. The constant suffering produced doubts in his mind about God. Questioning why the Lord allowed his sufferings to continue, Jeremiah began to doubt the Lord's faithfulness. God's promise seemed to be nothing more than a deceptive illusion (v. 18).

Honest complaints toward God may be the true reflection of your heart. Nevertheless, these complaints may also reveal sinful attitudes that require repentance. God cannot use a servant who does not trust Him in all His ways.

God, in His graciousness, called Jeremiah to repentance and restoration. The Lord chose Jeremiah, equipped him, and promised to be with him in all circumstances. The prophet needed to trust God and return to steadfastly proclaiming His messages. Notice that verse 20 recalls the Lord's promise to Jeremiah when He initially called him to service (1:18-19). God called on His prophet to repent of his sinful attitudes, then God recommissioned him to service.

"It's not about you." How many times have you heard that? Jeremiah had to come to that same realization in the midst of his personal pity party. It wasn't about his success or failure as a prophet, but rather about his obedience to speak God's truths to Judah.

Have you realized yet that your life in Christ isn't about your happiness, your accomplishments, or your satisfaction? If so, how did God reveal that to you? If you still struggle to understand that, what are some of your hangups?

Read Jeremiah 18:1-12,18.

As He did on other occasions with Jeremiah, the Lord used a symbolic action to send a message to Israel. God instructed Jeremiah to go to a potter's house. The Hebrew word for *potter* is derived from a verb that means "to make" or "to form." A form of the same verb occurs in Genesis 2:6, where it denotes God's creation of the first man's body from the dust of the ground. The imagery of the potter and the clay emphasizes the Lord's sovereignty over His people, and the importance of their submission to His will.

Jeremiah obeyed God and did as he was instructed. When he arrived at the potter's house, the potter was making a jar. But the jar he was making from clay became flawed. The Bible gives us no detail regarding the cause of this flaw. Maybe there were defects or contaminants in the clay. Perhaps the clay wasn't sufficiently moist or pliable. Though the clay was flawed, the potter didn't reject it. He continued working and made a jar.

Jeremiah's experience at the potter house reminds us that we are not hopeless when we fail God. No matter how we've blown it in the past, God can see beyond our flaws and failures to our future. The Lord can and will continue to work in us.

What is significant to you about the image of God as a potter? What changes do you need to make in order to cooperate with His efforts to mold you into the person He wants you to be?

The particular incident that prompted this symbolic message from God is not disclosed in the passage. However, it appears God zeroed in on the presumptive pride of the people. Having known of the Lord's intentions toward them expressed repeatedly through Abraham, Isaac, Jacob, and others through the ages, the people seemed to assume they were immune to any ill wind blowing in their direction. Their pride caused them to assume God's promise of blessing without recognizing their responsibility to live in right relationship with Him. God confronted that empty pride by assuring the nation He had the freedom to adjust His plan in response to the nation's turning toward or away from evil.

That God would "relent" from His plans (v. 10) causes some believers to struggle. The word literally means "to sigh" or "to breathe deeply," as if from a heart-felt grief. The picture is of God being deeply moved by our actions—either repentance or disobedience. When an individual or group repents of its sin and turns to God, God relents from the punishment He intended and welcomes the obedience.

Sadly, the people of Jeremiah's day did not repent. The prideful people would continue in their stubborn and evil ways (v. 12). Not only that, but the prophet's preaching kindled the anger of the religious establishment (v. 18). Earlier in Jeremiah's ministry, the men of Anathoth, Jeremiah's hometown, responded to Jeremiah's preaching with physical force, intending to kill him (11:18-23). Here, the religious leaders simply sought to destroy the prophet by discrediting him in the people's eyes. They would launch a propaganda campaign, thinking they could turn the tide of popular opinion against him.

When your pride and sin are challenged, are you more likely to repent or to seek to blame the messenger? Explain.

Jeremiah's ministry drew continual opposition that caused him constant pain. Gradually, the prophet lost patience with the nation. In 18:19-23, Jeremiah prayed against these foes, asking the Lord to punish their treachery. He told the people the truth, and in return they discredited and abused him. He grew tired of the very people he asked the Lord to spare. Yet Jeremiah did the right thing: instead of acting himself, he expressed his feelings to God and asked the Lord to deal with them.

What can we learn from Jeremiah about dealing with human opposition to our God-given ministry?

EZEKIEL

The Prophet to the Exiled

INTRODUCTION

Sometimes faith in God seems easy. Life proceeds smoothly, Christian friends surround us, and God's presence fills us. At other times faith in God becomes more difficult. Medical, financial, or spiritual problems invade our lives. Christian friends may abandon us, and God may seem distant. Faith and hope give way to fear and cynicism.

Ezekiel lived in difficult times. He was among the exiles from Judah, captured by Nebuchadnezzar and brought to Babylon as servants. Uprooted from his homeland at the age of twenty-five and marched off to a distant land, Ezekiel languished in despair for five years without a word from God. God seemed distant.

"The heavens were opened and I saw visions of God" (Ezek. 1:1). In a majestic vision of God's glory, Ezekiel discovered God was not distant, nor was the situation hopeless. While the Lord would punish His people because of their continued disobedience, He never abandoned them.

Ezekiel, whose name in Hebrew means "God strengthens," knew he had nothing personally to assist the exiles in their bitter situation. But he was convinced God's word spoke to their condition and could give them victory in it. Without question, the message that God gave Ezekiel served as a source of encouragement and hope to the exiles. Ezekiel's prophecies continue to encourage us that even in despair and defeat, we can affirm God's sovereign lordship.

How does God generally get your attention?

Why do you think God reveals Himself to different people in different ways?

*Watch the video teaching for Session 5 to discover "The World of Ezekiel,"
then continue the group discussion.*

FOCUS ATTENTION

Do you have an alarm system on your house or car? When has it scared someone away? When has it failed to work? Has it ever given false alarms?

EXPLORE THE TEXT

As a group, read Ezekiel 33:1-9.

What do we learn from verses 1-7 about the role of a watchman in ancient Israel? What could happen if the watchman didn't perform his job?

In what ways was Ezekiel to serve as a watchman (vv. 7-9)? What was the specific responsibility for which God would judge Ezekiel?

As a group, read Ezekiel 33:10-11.

What was the Lord's response to the people in verse 11? What does it reveal about God's character?

For what is God blamed in our day? How do these "accusations" hold up in light of verses 10-11?

As a group, read Ezekiel 33:30-33.

Where and why were people talking about Ezekiel? Why were they coming to hear him preach?

The good news in verses 30-33 was that the people were flocking to hear Ezekiel. What was the bad news?

Why do you think these people listened to Ezekiel's words but didn't change their ways? What do these verses tell us God values most?

APPLY THE TEXT

God appointed Ezekiel to be a watchman for the house of Israel. The issue wasn't whether Ezekiel was a watchman, but whether he would be a good one. God not only called him to a role, He also provided for his prophet the message—the word of the Lord (see Ezek. 33:7). Ezekiel was called to be a watchman, and so are we. We, too, have a word from the Lord that the world desperately needs to hear—the gospel of Jesus Christ.

In what sense are we the watchmen for our communities and cities? How is being watchful related to sharing the gospel?

For what reasons do Christians often resist the role of watchmen?

What are some practical ways you can be "on watch" this week?

Close your group time in prayer, reflecting on what you have discussed.

EZEKIEL

KEY VERSE

The appearance of the brilliant light all around was like that of a rainbow in a cloud on a rainy day. This was the appearance of the likeness of the LORD's glory. When I saw it, I fell facedown and heard a voice speaking.

— Ezekiel 1:28

BASIC FACTS

1. Sixth-century BC prophet who lived and prophesied in Babylon among the Jewish exile community.

2. Name *Ezekiel* means "God is my strength."

3. Taken along with 10,000 captives and King Jehoiachin from Jerusalem to Babylon in 597 BC; settled in area known as Chebar Canal.

4. Son of Buzi, who headed a priestly family in Jerusalem.

5. Called to be a prophet at age thirty after being in captivity for five years.

6. Married, but no known children; his wife—and probably Ezekiel—died in Babylon.

TIMELINE

600–500 BC

- Nebuchadnezzar takes Jehoiachin captive 597
- Ezekiel's prophetic ministry 593–570
- Jerusalem destroyed; people captured 586
- Temple of Solomon looted and burned 586
- Cyrus of Persia takes Babylon 539
- Edict of Cyrus allows Jews to return 539
- Second temple completed 515

500–400 BC

- Greeks defeat Persians at Marathon 490
- Esther becomes queen in Persia 479
- Golden age of Greek art 477–431
- Malachi's prophetic ministry 460 (early date)
- Jerusalem's wall rebuilt under Nehemiah 445
- Malachi's prophetic ministry 430 (late date)
- Old Testament biblical record falls silent 400

KNOWN FOR

1. Ezekiel came from an influential priestly family in Jerusalem and likely had begun serving in the temple priesthood. He was among the 10,000 leading Jews taken captive to Babylon with King Jehoiachin in 597 BC. God called Ezekiel while in Babylon to serve also as a prophet by giving him a number of key visionary revelations (Ezek. 1–3; 8–11; 37; 40–48).

2. Ezekiel's prophetic ministry was also characterized by sign, or acted, prophecies: eating a scroll (Ezek. 2:8–3:3); building a small brick model of a besieged Jerusalem and lying down beside the model for over a year (4:1-8); shaving his head and beard with a sword, then burning the hair (5:1-4); clapping his hands, stomping his feet, and singing taunt songs (6:11); displaying packed bags for exile (12:3-6); groaning bitterly in public (21:6-7); refusing to publicly mourn his wife's death (24:15-24); and writing on two sticks (37:15-28).

3. Ezekiel especially emphasized the Holy Spirit's role in revealing God's messages to His prophets. The Spirit initiated and explained Ezekiel's well-known prophecy concerning the reviving of dry bones into living people (Ezek. 37:1-14).

4. Ezekiel prophesied not only about the sinful rebellion of God's people, but also against the wicked nations that surrounded God's people (Ezek. 25–32).

400–200 BC	200–6 BC
Philip of Macedon conquers Greeks 338	Maccabees revolt against Antiochus IV 167
Alexander the Great defeats Persia 331	Jews gain independence 142–63
Greek world empire until Alexander dies 331–323	Roman general Pompey takes Holy Land 63
Greek empire divided: four generals 323	Herod the Great rules over Judea 37–4
Ptolemaic then Seleucid rule 323–168	John born to Zechariah and Elizabeth 6
Old Testament translated into Greek 250	Jesus born to the virgin Mary 6

Ezekiel: His Call and Message

By Harold R. Mosley

Ezekiel's visions, actions, and seemingly his personality were not the "normal" variety found among the prophets. The unusual nature of his prophecy causes some interpreters to avoid the book, while other interpreters engage in endless speculation about its meaning. Regardless of the book's difficulties, once the interpreter moves beyond the uniqueness of Ezekiel, his hard-hitting messages become evident.

The Inaugural Vision—Chapter 1

Ezekiel's inaugural vision echoes the temple vision of Isaiah 6. Both showed God seated upon a throne. The difficulty of understanding Ezekiel's vision is only partly due to the prophet's inability to describe God's glory in human terms. The prophet could not describe fully what he saw. Scattered throughout the chapter are the repetition of words such as "like," "appearance," "form," "shape," "wings," and "feet . . . like a calf." Are the creatures symbolic of something beyond the vision itself? Are they actual beings from the heavenly realm? What is the point of the vision? Understanding Ezekiel's Babylonian context can help in interpreting the vision.

Ezekiel was a captive in Babylon (see Ezek. 1:3). As such, he knew Mesopotamian culture. Statues of composite beasts had long been a feature of Mesopotamian history. These statues often consisted of the head of the king, the body of a lion or bull, and the wings of an eagle. The statues represented the kingdom's power and authority as well as the supposed gods' protection of the kingdom.

The essential focus of the vision is not the creatures, but the God who is above everything. God's power is never threatened by human kingdoms. Although Ezekiel lived among an exiled people, God was still in control. This was important for Ezekiel to know, since God called him to minister to a defeated and discouraged people. Isaiah, Jeremiah, and Daniel also emphasized God's control of human history.

The Call—Chapter 2

A prophet spoke what God revealed. The messages the prophets received were based on the only Scripture available to them, that is, God's Law, or Torah. The prophets drew their messages from the covenant God made with Israel at Sinai. Most often, a

Harold R. Mosley, "Ezekiel: His Call and Message," *Biblical Illustrator,* Summer 2014.

ILLUSTRATOR PHOTO/ DAVID ROGERS (7/8/4) | ILLUSTRATOR PHOTO/ MURRAY SEVERANCE (74/1/11)

prophet preached not a new message but an application in his context of the blessings or judgments of the covenant's obligations.

Ezekiel's call consisted of God putting His words into the prophet's mouth, though, as was typical for Ezekiel, the method was unusual. God commanded Ezekiel to eat a scroll containing words and speak the words to the nation (2:8–3:4).

The Task—Chapter 3

God sent Ezekiel to his own people. With this call came the realization that the people would not listen to Ezekiel, because they would not listen to God (v. 7). A watchman's task compels him to warn the city of danger. Ezekiel similarly had to warn his people, whether they responded or not (vv. 16-21). God controls human history for His own purpose, and He invites humans to respond to Him in faith and obedience. That was Ezekiel's message. It is still God's message to us today.

Nebuchadnezzar II built the famous Ishtar Gate and the Procession Street in ancient Babylon. Magnificent enamel tiles covered mud-brick walls picturing steers, lions, and dragons. Tops of walls were crenellated to form battlements or protection for soldiers from arrows and stones.

Young man sitting under a palm canopy beside the river in Babylon. The Lord appeared to Ezekiel while he was "among the exiles by the Chebar Canal" (Ezek. 1:1).

Read Ezekiel 1:1-3; 2:1-7.

Ezekiel's prophetic ministry began at a time when he and his people were in the throws of devastating circumstances. Life was hard and hope, perhaps, was gone. Far from their homeland of Judah, they lived as captives in the "land of the Chaldeans" (Ezek. 1:3). "Chaldeans" was another name for the Babylonians.

Conquered by the powerful Babylonian army, the Israelites were cut off from their home and stripped of their freedom. But God showed up and demonstrated to Ezekiel that he could rely on the Lord in these darkest hours and find a purpose in the depths of his pain.

Most Jews believed God lived in the temple in Jerusalem. When the Lord appeared to Ezekiel in Babylon (Ezek. 1:3), what must Ezekiel and the other exiles have realized about God?

A priest displaced from his home and place of service, Ezekiel found himself living in a state of crisis just like the rest of the captives. In times of crisis, we often move from living for a purpose to just trying to survive. God's call on Ezekiel's life at this particular time demonstrates God still has a purpose for us when unexpected circumstances sidetrack our lives.

You may not have a clue what it's like to live in captivity, exiled from your homeland and stripped of your freedom. But chances are, you're no stranger to crisis. Determine now that you will seek God's presence and purpose in your day of trouble. Begin investing daily time in cultivating your relationship with Him, so you'll already be close when you need to turn to Him.

God's purpose for Ezekiel was to speak His message to rebellious Israel. The Lord didn't promise Ezekiel this would be an easy task, nor did He promise a favorable outcome. But He did give His prophet the power to carry out what He called him to do.

The Lord addressed Ezekiel as "Son of man" (2:1), emphasizing the prophet's weakness. It draws a distinction between the frailness of mortal humanity compared to the eternal majesty of Almighty God. The Lord reminded the prophet of his weaknesses and frailties, but He also reminded him that He, the Lord, was neither weak nor frail. The Spirit of God came upon Ezekiel to enable and empower him for the improbable mission God presented him.

God's assignment would be a tough one. The Lord acknowledged He was sending Ezekiel to a rebellious, obstinate, and hardhearted people (vv. 3-4) but instructed His prophet not to be afraid of them (v. 6). God commanded Ezekiel to speak the truth— whether the people listened or refused to listen (vv. 4-5). He just needed to keep doing and saying right things and leave the results to God. This would be the measure of his success from God's perspective.

Why did Ezekiel need to clearly understand his mission before he could succeed?

Who have you (perhaps subconsciously) labeled a "lost cause" spiritually? Why should we never feel defeated when we witness, according to Ezekiel 2:5?

Attempting to minister in the name of Jesus can be an intimidating task. From where do Christians find strength to minister to others or to share our faith? Believers today enjoy the continual presence of the indwelling Holy Spirit. God will strengthen believers to do His work, even in times of crises or when the response may be disappointing.

Read Ezekiel 33:7-11,30-33.

Ezekiel 33 was written in a time when watchmen guarded cities. These guards stood atop city walls and watched the surrounding countryside for signs of an enemy invasion. If foreign troops were spotted, the watchman had a duty to blow a trumpet and warn the inhabitants of the city to flee or prepare for battle.

God compared this duty to the one he'd given His prophet. Ezekiel was to be God's watchman who warned the Israelites of God's coming judgment. If the people repented, good. If they didn't repent and were destroyed, Ezekiel wouldn't be held responsible. A watchman was guilty of the blood of those who perished if an attack came and the people were not warned, but he was guiltless if the alarm was sounded and no one responded.

How do Christians today serve as watchmen like Ezekiel? For whom are you responsible, and for what are you watching?

Warning others of the consequences of sin is never a popular assignment. Nonetheless, believers have a duty to be "watchmen" who warn people of the destructive nature of sin. Our responsibility is to warn and proclaim as persuasively as possible, but how the message is received is beyond our control.

Ezekiel had faithfully proclaimed God's coming judgment on the sins of Israel (see 7:1-9; 18:30-32), and the judgment had come. In 587 BC, Nebuchadnezzar, king of Babylon, conquered Judah and destroyed Jerusalem. Previously, the people had put the blame for their predicaments on their fathers (18:1-3) and even on God (18:25). But when God's judgment on Israel became a reality, the exiles accepted their responsibility for the fall of their nation (33:10-11). It's unfortunate that most people see no need to turn from their wrong ways unless they experience the consequences firsthand.

Ezekiel assured the Israelites that God would forgive them if they would turn from their sin and repent. "Why will you die?" the prophet asked them (v. 11). God wants all people to live. That's why He sent Jesus to die on the cross for our sins.

Sometime after Ezekiel's call to repent, news arrived in Babylon that Judah had fallen and Jerusalem had been destroyed (vv. 21-22). This fulfillment of Ezekiel's prophecy of Jerusalem's destruction had a powerful impact on the exiles. They mourned for the loss of their city, but likewise marveled at Ezekiel's God-given ability to prophesy about the future. Overnight, Ezekiel became a celebrity.

God put Ezekiel's popularity into true perspective. Even though the exiles came to Ezekiel in crowds and hung on his every word, the Lord warned the prophet his preaching had not penetrated his audience. Ezekiel's audience came to listen out of curiosity rather than to be changed through God's word. They appreciated Ezekiel's entertainment value but had no intention of repenting and turning to God.

Each Sunday morning in churches across our country, many people come to hear the Lord's message through His messengers. Many pastors preach God's Word boldly, and as people file out they say, "I really enjoyed that sermon." But do they really take the message to heart?

What can you do to make sure you don't just hear God's Word but also put it into practice?

We don't want to make the same mistake the Israelites made and pretend we're interested in what God wants while our hearts are consumed with other things. Remember, it isn't enough to hear God's warning or to believe God's promise and enjoy a good worship service. We please God when we obey Him, and He is calling us now to repent of our sins and to help others do the same.

Read Ezekiel 37:1-14, 23-24.

Ezekiel 37 opens with one of the most fascinating stories in the Old Testament. God brought Ezekiel to a valley filled with human bones that were very dry—indicating they had been there for a long time. Symbolically, these bones represented the spiritual deadness of the people.

Any suggestion that there could ever again be life in the dried up bones would appear preposterous. Yet, as Ezekiel surveyed the scene, he heard a question: "Son of man, can these bones live?" (v. 3). The prophet's restrained answer was filled with his awareness of human helplessness in the face of death, but also respect for the mystery of God's power. He knew that if the bones could live, it was a matter only God knew and the giving of life was a deed only God could perform. Consequently, when God told him to preach to the dry bones, Ezekiel obeyed despite its apparent absurdity. The message he was to deliver was a simple one, "Dry bones, hear the word of the LORD!" (v. 4). The Lord would give breath, life, tendons, flesh, and skin to these bones so they would know that He is the Lord.

Ezekiel's obedience produced immediate results. Even before he finished speaking, he heard the noise of the fulfillment of God's promise (v. 7). The bones came together and were clothed with flesh but still were not alive (v. 8). So God again commanded the prophet to preach to the "breath" (v. 9). The imperative to "breathe" is the same verb used in the creation account of Genesis 2:7. It clearly was God's Spirit who was to give breath to these corpses. Ezekiel preached to the "breath," and life entered these corpses, and they stood as a vast, living, reconstituted army (v. 10).

God then interpreted Ezekiel's vision. The bones of Ezekiel's vision symbolized the house of Israel (v. 11). This was a picture of the restoration of the nation that God would bring about. God promised to bring the exiles out of Babylon, lead them back to the land of Israel (vv. 12-13), and put His Spirit in them (v. 14). Then they would know that God is the Lord.

After the destruction of Jerusalem, the Israelites believed the nation had dried up like the bones in Ezekiel's vision. The dry bones depicted the death and hopelessness of the nation. Their hope had perished long ago. They would have stood alongside Ezekiel, seen the same vision, heard the initial question of the Lord, and responded with mocking laughter. Nothing in life seems as hopeless as death. However, the Lord revealed to Ezekiel that indeed these dry bones could and would live.

Ezekiel's prophecy looked beyond the restoration of the Israelites to their own land. He anticipated the new life that would come in the Messiah, Jesus Christ (v. 24). Israel's restoration was not just about rescue; it was about rebirth that would result in a change of heart from rebellion and idolatry to submission and obedience (v. 23).

What lessons can you learn from Ezekiel's vision of the valley of dry bones?

Many people live with a belief that God either doesn't care about them or He doesn't have the power to save them. In the same way God promised new life for the people of Israel, we can be confident that He offers to all people today new life in Christ.

According to Ephesians 2:1, people who don't know Jesus as Savior are like the dry bones of Ezekiel's vision. How is spiritual life possible? (See Ephesians 2:4-9.)

Ezekiel's vision means that in God there is hope for new life—even when life feels like a valley of dead, dried up bones. Jesus taught that with God all things are possible (Matt. 19:26). As believers, we can assure those who feel hopeless that God does care, and He is able to save them.

Whose spiritual "bones" are you praying to see revived today? How does knowing you have a God who can do the impossible give you hope?

MALACHI

The Purifying Prophet

INTRODUCTION

What would you say to an individual who questioned God's love? How might you challenge the person who serves God but gives less than his best? Or what message would you deliver to the person who says there's nothing to be gained in serving God?

Malachi spoke God's message to a people who were saying and doing all of the above. About a hundred years after the Jews were permitted to return from exile to Judah, much of Jerusalem was still in ruins. The better times promised by earlier prophets had not come as the people expected. Many began to doubt God and lose their faith. Worship became drudgery. Priests taught false doctrine, not the true instruction from the Lord. Husbands divorced their wives and married pagan women. People refused to support the Lord's house with their tithes. Some even asserted that serving God was a waste of time.

Into that scene of spiritual apathy and rebellion, Malachi spoke God's message. Not surprisingly, he began by challenging their concept of God. Malachi knew that when people see God for who He really is, they will give Him their best.

Have you ever developed a spirit of indifference about something? How did you deal with it?

In what ways can ceremony take the place of sincere love?

Watch the video teaching for Session 6 to discover "The World of Malachi,"
then continue the group discussion.

FOCUS ATTENTION

When have you had to deliver a difficult message? How did it go? How did the recipient(s) receive the message?

EXPLORE THE TEXT

As a group, read Malachi 1:1-2.

The Lord begins this book with a declaration of His love. How did God reassure the people of His love? What does this say about God's love for us?

As a group, read Malachi 1:6-8.

What did God call Himself (besides "Lord of Hosts") in verse 6? To whom was He speaking? What was God saying by using these metaphors?

How did the priests in Malachi's day despise God's name? What did they offer to God that they wouldn't dare offer to their governor? What warning can we find in this for our own lives?

As a group, read Malachi 1:9-11.

Look at verses 9-10. What was God's response to the sacrifices of His people? What would God rather have happen if the people continued to give less than their best?

What does verse 11 say about God? In light of what it says about Him, what does it affirm about the priests?

As a group, read Malachi 1:12-14.

According to verse 13, how did the priests feel about offering sacrifices? How can we apply this to our own worship?

Do you think people today try to "con" or deceive God? Explain.

APPLY THE TEXT

Malachi clearly was a man of great courage. He was willing to speak out against the religious establishment on some sensitive subjects. Without a doubt, the words God spoke through His prophet in the fifth century BC are apt for us today. God seeks worshipers who worship Him with their whole hearts. When we just go through the motions and give the Lord second best, we dishonor Him and deceive ourselves.

What does your attitude toward worship say about your relationship with God?

In what ways can you honor God with your life and demonstrate wholehearted love for Him?

Close your group time in prayer, reflecting on what you have discussed.

MALACHI

KEY VERSE

"See, I am going to send my messenger, and he will clear the way before me. Then the Lord you seek will suddenly come to his temple, the Messenger of the covenant you delight in—see, he is coming," says the Lord of Armies.

— Malachi 3:1

BASIC FACTS

1. Fifth-century BC prophet of the Lord to the restored Jewish community in Judah.

2. Name *Malachi* means "my messenger."

3. Family lineage unknown; a contemporary of Ezra and Nehemiah.

4. Writer of the last prophetic book in the Old Testament.

TIMELINE

600–500 BC

- Nebuchadnezzar takes Jehoiachin captive 597
- Ezekiel's prophetic ministry 593–570
- Jerusalem destroyed; people captured 586
- Temple of Solomon looted and burned 586
- Cyrus of Persia takes Babylon 539
- Edict of Cyrus allows Jews to return 539
- Second temple completed 515

500–400 BC

- Greeks defeat Persians at Marathon 490
- Esther becomes queen in Persia 479
- Golden age of Greek art 477–431
- Malachi's prophetic ministry 460 (early date)
- Jerusalem's wall rebuilt under Nehemiah 445
- Malachi's prophetic ministry 430 (late date)
- Old Testament biblical record falls silent 400

KNOWN FOR

1. Malachi is known for his question-and-answer preaching style. He posed more than twenty-five questions in his book as a way of leading God's people into honest reflection and repentance.

2. He recognized that the post-exilic Jewish community—both priests and people—had lapsed into serious spiritual rebellion. Too many priests were corrupt (Mal. 1:6–2:9). Too many Jewish men were divorcing their wives and marrying younger foreign women (2:10-16). Too many worshipers refused to support God's work through tithes and offerings (3:7-12). And too many of God's people doubted God and spoke against Him (3:13-15).

3. Malachi included at least three messianic references in his writing (Mal. 3:1; 4:2-3,5-6).

4. Malachi is often referred to as the last prophet of the Old Testament era. Jesus alluded to Malachi 4:5 in describing John the Baptist as the "Elijah who is to come" (Matt. 11:14).

400–200 BC	200–6 BC
Philip of Macedon conquers Greeks 338	Maccabees revolt against Antiochus IV 167
Alexander the Great defeats Persia 331	Jews gain independence 142–63
Greek world empire until Alexander dies 331–323	Roman general Pompey takes Holy Land 63
Greek empire divided: four generals 323	Herod the Great rules over Judea 37–4
Ptolemaic then Seleucid rule 323–168	John born to Zechariah and Elizabeth 6
Old Testament translated into Greek 250	Jesus born to the virgin Mary 6

An Overview of Malachi

By E. Ray Clendenen

At the end of the Old Testament era, Malachi confronted three problems. First, the priests no longer served God wholeheartedly or the people conscientiously (Mal. 1:2–2:9). Second, the people were living selfish lives and ignoring their responsibilities to God and one another (2:10–3:6). Third, the people also had a self-protective sense of ownership of their personal property (3:7–4:6). Malachi confronted these problems in three addresses.

First Address

Malachi declared God's love for His people (1:2-5). Yet life's trials had blinded them to His faithfulness and presence. The resultant spiritual impoverishment led to Israel's offensive religious rites, moral decay, and spiritual indifference.

Malachi instructed the priests to honor God (1:2–2:9). He described their offering unsatisfactory sacrifices, which the Lord commanded them to stop giving (1:6-10). The priests' careless attitude betrayed how the people disregarded their relationship with God. Malachi also described how the priests' worship was profaning the Lord's name (1:11-14). Malachi ended this address by telling the priests God would thus remove them disgracefully from service (2:1-9).

Second Address

Malachi began his second address by instructing the people to be faithful to one another (2:10–3:6). The people were violating their responsibilities to others and acting faithlessly (2:10-15a). This included Jewish men, who divorced their Jewish wives in order to marry pagan women who worshiped foreign gods. God condemned such men, saying their actions were like a stained garment for all to see (2:16).

Yet the people were complaining of the Lord's injustice (v. 17). God's reply was to announce a coming messenger of judgment who would purify God's people (3:1-6). God's "messenger" here was the "voice . . . in the wilderness" (Isa. 40:3), which the New Testament interprets as the "Elijah" of Malachi 4:5, fulfilled (provisionally) by John the Baptist. He would call people to repent and prepare for God's ultimate "Messenger," the Messiah.

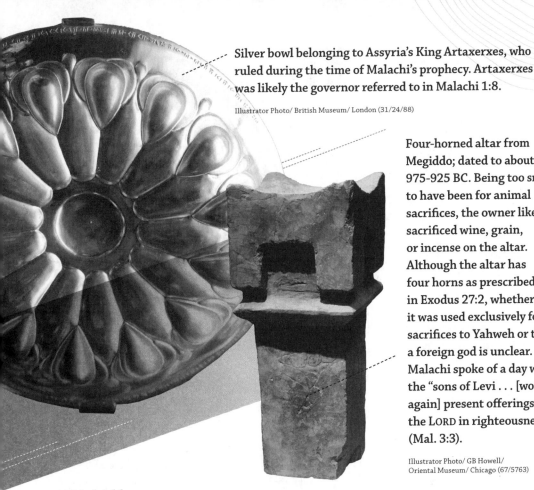

Silver bowl belonging to Assyria's King Artaxerxes, who ruled during the time of Malachi's prophecy. Artaxerxes was likely the governor referred to in Malachi 1:8.

Illustrator Photo/ British Museum/ London (31/24/88)

Four-horned altar from Megiddo; dated to about 975-925 BC. Being too small to have been for animal sacrifices, the owner likely sacrificed wine, grain, or incense on the altar. Although the altar has four horns as prescribed in Exodus 27:2, whether it was used exclusively for sacrifices to Yahweh or to a foreign god is unclear. Malachi spoke of a day when the "sons of Levi . . . [would again] present offerings to the LORD in righteousness" (Mal. 3:3).

Illustrator Photo/ GB Howell/ Oriental Museum/ Chicago (67/5763)

Third Address

In his final address (Mal. 3:7–4:6), Malachi strongly urged Israel to "Return" and "Remember." He commanded them to return to God with tithes (3:7-10a), thereby acknowledging His ownership of all they had and His faithfulness.

Being complacent toward serving God kept people from repenting (3:13-15). The coming day of the Lord, though, motivated them to repent and obey (3:16–4:3). God promised He would come with compassion to retrieve all who serve Him (3:17).

God promised to redemptively invade this world of darkness with "righteousness" as the "sun" invades the night (4:2). God will bring healing to His children. Fathers and children will no longer live self-serving lives but will regard one another with compassion and respect.

Malachi's messages are as relevant today as they were centuries ago. God's love demands that we love and worship Him with all our hearts, that we reproduce His love in our relationships, and that we acknowledge His ownership of all we have.

E. Ray Clendenen, "An Overview of Malachi," *Biblical Illustrator*, Summer 2012.

Read Malachi 1:1-14.

We know very little about the man Malachi. He was God's messenger to speak to the people of Jerusalem in the fifth century BC. Several decades had passed since the Israelites were permitted to return home from captivity in Babylon. The temple was completed, but Jerusalem was in bad shape. Economic conditions were poor. Parents sold their children into slavery to pay debts (Neh. 5:5). Revenue for the temple was so low the Levites moved into the country to make their living farming (Neh. 13:10). Faith gave way to doubt and skepticism. The people ignored God's commands. They neglected worship or offered unacceptable sacrifices when they did attend.

Very little is known about Malachi the man. The book that bears his name is about the message, not the messenger. Why is that significant?

Malachi's message begins with an emphasis on God's love for His people (Mal. 1:2). Many Israelites questioned God's love due to their hardships and the conditions in their country. God answered their cynicism by affirming His love and reminding them why they were His covenant people: He had chosen them. They were descendants of Jacob, the twin brother of Esau. Of the two, God chose Jacob, not Esau (who was born first), to be the father of His special people. God's choice of Jacob and his descendants, not Esau and his descendants, demonstrated His love for the nation Israel.

Have you ever asked God to prove His love to you? What evidence has God given that He loves you?

It's important that we understand God not only loved Israel, He loves every one of us as well. He demonstrated His love for us by sending His Son, Jesus Christ, to make it possible for us to have a relationship with Him (see Rom. 5:8).

Following the affirmation of His love, God accused Israel's priests of disrespecting Him. They didn't even give Him the honor a son should give his father or a servant his master (v. 6). When they asked how they had dishonored Him, God pointed to the defiled sacrifices they offered on the altar—blind, lame, and sick animals. These gifts revealed how little God meant to them (v. 8). The people went through the motions of religious ritual but failed in the deeper aspects of worship. God told them they might as well shut the temple doors if they were going to continue these irreverent practices (v. 10).

God had established Israel to carry His name to all the people of the earth so that all nations might turn to Him and worship Him. Unlike the Israelites' impure sacrifices, God wanted pure offerings of worship in every place. God's name would be magnified among the nations (v. 11).

God told the priests what was wrong with the offerings they were accepting from the people and sacrificing to Him (vv. 12-14). The Lord's requirements had become burdensome to them; they viewed the entire process as a nuisance. They considered only what benefit they received from worship rather than how God might be glorified.

In what way does the quality of the gift you give someone reflect the quality of your love for that person? What do your gifts to God communicate?

We too can be guilty of offering God blemished sacrifices—giving Him second best and holding back the best for ourselves. We too may evaluate worship by how it meets our expectations and desires, and not by how it glorifies God. We try to fit God into our schedules instead of giving Him our lives. Don't be guilty of offering God less than your best.

Read Malachi 2:10-17.

At what point in your life did you realize that actions and choices have consequences? Many people in today's world believe they can live their lives with impunity. They fail to understand God has clear laws that transcend every culture and nation. When those laws are disobeyed, consequences follow. The Israelites of Malachi's day had to learn this important lesson.

In the Ten Commandments, the Lord laid down the terms of His covenant relationship with Israel (see Ex. 20:1-20). The rest of the law describes finer points as well as examples of the covenant's application in real-life scenarios. The problem in Malachi's time, as perhaps today, wasn't that the people didn't know the terms of God's covenant. The problem was that they ignored or trivialized its terms. They willfully broke the covenant, putting themselves in danger of the consequences.

Malachi 2:3-7 references the covenant God made with Levi and his descendants when He chose them to be His priests. They were to have reverence for God, instruct the people in the ways of God, and walk in those ways themselves. The priests of Malachi's day had departed from that kind of ministry.

These priests caused many to stumble by their poor example (vv. 8-9). This reminds us that we do not live in a vacuum. When we live selfishly, our actions can have a negative impact on others. When we live faithfully for God, we can have a greater impact for good than we realize. Think about the impact Malachi, Ezra, and Nehemiah had on the people of their generation and even today.

Have you ever heard anyone use the statement, "What I do is my own business"? Do you think this is true? Why or why not? How does this passage apply to that discussion?

Malachi turned from addressing the priests to addressing the people living in Jerusalem. God called them to set godly examples in their obligations to one another and especially in their marriage relationships. People were violating God's covenant by intermarrying with foreign wives who worshiped idols (v. 11). The danger of intermarrying with idol-worshiping peoples was obvious: God's people would become entangled in idolatry themselves.

Those to whom Malachi prophesied claimed ignorance in the face of the Lord's accusations. They asked, "Why?" (Mal. 2:14). The answer, Malachi replied, lay in the broken state of their marital relationships. To marry pagan women, some men were divorcing their wives—women to whom they had been married for many years. These husbands were breaking faith with their wives and with the God of the covenant. The Lord's plan is for husbands and wives to live faithfully with each other and with Him.

Malachi encouraged married believers to be faithful to the vows they made to God and to one another. God desires for us to keep our marriage vows and to do the hard and unceasing work of building and maintaining a strong, healthy, godly marriage relationship.

How is your commitment to God reflected in your relationships with others?

Malachi reminds us that our lifestyles and life choices are to honor the Lord. Honoring the Lord involves not only believing, but also standing for God's unchanging truth. If we want to bear the Lord's name so that He is glorified, we will keep our commitments to God and also to other people.

Read Malachi 3:1-18.

According to Malachi, a question we need to ask is what God wants of us when we worship. Our worship is acceptable to Him only when we worship in ways that bring honor to His name.

The inappropriate worship practices of Malachi's day were a reflection of the people's hearts. They not only questioned God's love for them, they questioned God's goodness and fairness. From their perspective, it seemed that evil people were prospering, while they remained mired in difficult times. They were asking one another, "Where is the God of justice?" (see 2:17).

The Lord answered through His prophet Malachi, but not in the way they had hoped. God promised to send His messenger who would restore hope and purity to His people. This messenger would lead people to turn from their sins. Who would this messenger be? More than 400 years after Malachi, Jesus identified that messenger as John the Baptist, who came to prepare the way for Jesus by preaching about repentance and the forgiveness of sins (Matt. 11:11-14).

Malachi also told of a second messenger who would come after the first prepared the way. The second messenger is described as "the Lord" and a "Messenger of the covenant" (Mal. 3:1). This referred to Jesus, who came to establish a new covenant through His blood (Matt. 26:28).

Many Israelites pictured the Lord returning as a victorious king who would destroy all their enemies. Malachi informed them that the Lord would indeed come to render justice, but not only to Israel's enemies. He would pass judgment on all people—including the priests and the people of Israel. His coming would be like a "refiner's fire" and a cleansing soap (Mal. 3:2-3). After the Lord's purifying process, the priests and the people would then be able to present offerings that would please the Lord because they were cleansed from their sins.

What in your life needs to be refined and cleansed to restore a right relationship with God? How willing are you to give up everything that stands in the way of your worshiping Him with genuineness and sincerity?

Though Malachi prophesied that God would judge Israel (v. 5), this didn't mean the end for them. God had made covenant promises about His people's future. God is always dependable and trustworthy. His promises are sure. We don't have to be afraid that God might one day be different from what He has always been. Paul wrote, "If we are faithless, he remains faithful, for he cannot deny himself" (2 Tim. 2:13).

The Lord still loved His people, despite their unfaithfulness, and wanted them to return to Him. If they would repent of their sins, His blessings would again rest on the nation. The people asked Malachi how they could return to God (Mal. 3:7). That's what Malachi had been trying to tell them throughout this entire book! Genuine worship was a theme of Malachi's message, and here he explained that tithes and offerings are one aspect of genuine worship.

If the people would trust God in the area of giving, they would experience God's blessings. These blessings may be material, but they can also be spiritual. We give to Him out of love, not because of what we think we might receive in return.

The current bad economic situation in Judah led some people to conclude it was useless to worship and serve God (Mal. 3:14-15). Their attitude was, "What's in it for me?" These were the same people who claimed to have faithfully carried out God's requirements!

Why is serving God worthwhile?

In contrast to the skeptics who saw no value in serving or worshiping God, there were still some people who had a genuine reverence for the Lord and who paid attention to Malachi's messages. What about you? Do you approach worship with a "what's in it for me" attitude? Do you simply go through the motions of worship, or does your worship reflect a heart that truly loves the Lord?

TIPS FOR LEADING A SMALL GROUP

Follow these guidelines to prepare for each group session.

PRAYERFULLY PREPARE

Review

Review the weekly material and group questions ahead of time.

Pray

Be intentional about praying for each person in the group. Ask the Holy Spirit to work through you and the group discussion as you point to Jesus each week through God's Word.

MINIMIZE DISTRACTIONS

Create a comfortable environment. If group members are uncomfortable, they'll be distracted and therefore not engaged in the group experience. Plan ahead by considering these details:

Seating

Temperature

Lighting

Food or Drink

Surrounding Noise

General Cleanliness

At best, thoughtfulness and hospitality show guests and group members they're welcome and valued in whatever environment you choose to gather. At worst, people may never notice your effort, but they're also not distracted. Do everything in your ability to help people focus on what's most important: connecting with God, with the Bible, and with one another.

INCLUDE OTHERS

Your goal is to foster a community in which people are welcome just as they are but encouraged to grow spiritually. Always be aware of opportunities to include any people who visit the group and to invite new people to join your group. An inexpensive way to make first-time guests feel welcome or to invite someone to get involved is to give them their own copies of this Bible study book.

ENCOURAGE DISCUSSION

A good small-group experience has the following characteristics.

Everyone Participates

Encourage everyone to ask questions, share responses, or read aloud.

No One Dominates—Not Even the Leader

Be sure that your time speaking as a leader takes up less than half of your time together as a group. Politely guide discussion if anyone dominates.

Nobody Is Rushed Through Questions

Don't feel that a moment of silence is a bad thing. People often need time to think about their responses to questions they've just heard or to gain courage to share what God is stirring in their hearts.

Input Is Affirmed and Followed Up

Make sure you point out something true or helpful in a response. Don't just move on. Build community with follow-up questions, asking how other people have experienced similar things or how a truth has shaped their understanding of God and the Scripture you're studying. People are less likely to speak up if they fear that you don't actually want to hear their answers or that you're looking for only a certain answer.

God and His Word Are Central

Opinions and experiences can be helpful, but God has given us the truth. Trust God's Word to be the authority and God's Spirit to work in people's lives. You can't change anyone, but God can. Continually point people to the Word and to active steps of faith.

HOW TO USE THE LEADER GUIDE

PREPARE TO LEAD

Each session of the Leader Guide is designed to be torn out so you, the leader, can have this front-and-back page with you as you lead your group through the session. Watch the session teaching video and read through the session content with the Leader Guide tear-out in hand and notice how it supplements each section of the study.

FOCUS ATTENTION

These questions are provided to help get the discussion started. They are generally more introductory and topical in nature.

EXPLORE THE TEXT

Questions in this section have some sample answers or discussion prompts provided in the Leader Guide, if needed, to help you jump-start or steer the conversation.

APPLY THE TEXT

This section contains questions that allow group members an opportunity to apply the content they have been discussing together.

BIOGRAPHY AND FURTHER INSIGHT MOMENT

These sections aren't covered in the leader guide and may be used during the group session or by group members as a part of the personal study time during the week. If you choose to use them during your group session, make sure you are familiar with the content and how you intend to use it before your group meets.

Conclude each group session with a prayer.

SESSION 1 | LEADER GUIDE

FOCUS ATTENTION

Elijah withstood the pressure to compromise his personal convictions. Describe a time when you felt pressured to conform in order to "fit in." How did you respond?

- All Christians will feel the pressure to compromise biblical values and conform to culture's values. They will face the decision whether or not to take a bold stand for God.

EXPLORE THE TEXT

Ask a volunteer to read 1 Kings 18:17-21.

If a modern-day Elijah was speaking to our culture, how do you think he might express his challenge in verse 21?

- The challenge Elijah faced was establishing that God is the only God rather than one among many. Our challenge is somewhat different: establishing the reality of the one God in the minds of people who live without any idea of God or who allow their personal preferences to become god in their lives.

Why didn't the people say anything in response to Elijah's challenge?

- Some of the Israelites may have known the Lord was God but chose the sinful pleasures that idolatry offered. Some may have felt no need or desire to make a choice; they thought they could serve both Baal and God.

Ask a volunteer to read 1 Kings 18:22-24.

What was Elijah hoping to accomplish by establishing the contest with the prophets of Baal?

- The contest would show the people who truly ruled Israel—the Baals of Ahab and Jezebel or the Lord. Baal was reputed to be the god of storm, and therefore should at least have been able to bring down fire (lightning).

- The contest also would show who was the one ruining Israel—the rebellious king Ahab or Elijah, the Lord's prophet.

What does Elijah's challenge to the prophets of Baal say about the nature of faith?

- Elijah was willing to act on his faith.

- Faith involves risk.

- There comes a time when private faith must be lived out publicly.

Ask a volunteer to read 1 Kings 18:25-29.

What actions did the prophets of Baal take to try to persuade their god to send fire? What additional insights about the nature of faith do we learn from their actions?

- The prophets of Baal were zealous in their devotion to their god, but they had a misplaced faith.

- Much faith in a non-existent god is no faith at all, while a little faith in the true God is great faith indeed.

Ask a volunteer to read 1 Kings 18:36-39.

How did Elijah's prayer contrast with the prayers of the prophets of Baal? What is significant about this?

- Elijah did not attempt to coax the Lord nor seek to convince him. Rather, in complete confidence, he addressed his prayer to the covenant God.

- Elijah showed by his prayer that his foremost concerns were God's glory and the people's relationship with God.

Does God answer prayers today like He did those of Elijah? Should we expect God's miraculous intervention as was shown in Elijah's situation?

- James cited an example from Elijah's ministry to encourage his readers to expect God to answer their prayers (see Jas. 5:13-18).

- We should never put limits on God or deny that He can do anything He chooses.

- We should not make demands on God. Our role is to trust in the Lord and live in conscious dependence on Him. This will require us to take bold stands and trust God with the outcome.

APPLY THE TEXT

What's the main point of the story—what Elijah did for God or what God did through Elijah? Why does it matter that we understand the difference?

When you are confronted with differing viewpoints about God, what do you tend to do? What would it mean for you to follow Elijah's example?

How can the story of Elijah encourage and prepare you for the time when the Lord asks you to do something that will require a bold step of faith?

SESSION 2 | LEADER GUIDE

FOCUS ATTENTION

What excuses do you typically use to justify disobedience to God?

- Some claim they want to know God's will but resist carrying out His clear directives when they learn God's will differs from their personal preferences.

EXPLORE THE TEXT

Ask a volunteer to read Jonah 1:1-3.

What was God's assignment for Jonah? How did Jonah respond?

- God instructed Jonah to go to Nineveh, the capital city of the Assyrians.
- Jonah had no desire to be a missionary to the evil people of Nineveh. He got on a ship headed for Tarshish, probably a Phoenician seaport in Spain. Tarshish was about as far as Jonah could get from Nineveh in those days.

What was Jonah trying to accomplish by fleeing to Tarshish? What do you suppose he was thinking as he boarded the ship?

- While Jonah likely knew he couldn't escape from God, he hated Nineveh and wasn't inclined to do anything that might save the Ninevites from God's wrath.

Ask a volunteer to read Jonah 1:4,7-12.

What's ironic about what Jonah told the sailors concerning himself and God? How did his actions and words contradict one another? Why are both actions and words important in sharing God's message?

- Jonah confessed that he worshiped the God who created everything. His profession revealed his understanding and affirmation of God's sovereignty, although his actions contradicted his beliefs. Even the unbelieving sailors could see the foolishness of Jonah's attempt to get beyond the reach of God.

Do you think Jonah's request to be thrown into the sea reflected God's will, or was that still Jonah being rebellious? Explain your answer.

- The text gives no evidence of Jonah's repentance or a change of heart. He was trying to escape the Lord's mission, if not to Tarshish then to a watery grave.

Ask a volunteer to read 1:17–2:4,9-10.

Were God's actions in verse 17 a demonstration of His judgment or His mercy? How was Jonah finally showing some sense?

- That the Lord appointed a huge fish to swallow Jonah shows He was still actively pursuing His prophet.

- This is the first time in the biblical account that Jonah actually prayed.

Ask a volunteer to read Jonah 3:1-5.

How did Jonah respond to God's command this time? What message from God did Jonah preach in Nineveh? What do you find unusual about Jonah's sermon?

- We are not told whether Jonah's attitude toward the Ninevites had softened. Regardless, he now acted in obedience to the Lord's command. Compassion could develop in time; obedience was step one.

- Jonah preached that destruction was coming in forty days.

Ask a volunteer to read Jonah 3:10–4:11.

What was the intent of God's confronting Jonah with the question in verse 4?

- Jonah's anger was inappropriate; God wanted to help His prophet understand His compassion for all people, not just for the people of Israel.

- Do we ever think as Jonah did? Are there some people in the world we have difficulty viewing with compassion?

How did God teach Jonah a lesson about His compassion for lost people?

- God used a plant that shaded Jonah to teach him about having compassion for Nineveh. Jonah was more concerned about a plant than the destruction of 120,000 people.

- Just as God did with sinners from the earliest times of the human race (see Gen. 3:11; 4:9), He forced Jonah to admit his sin through the use of a question.

APPLY THE TEXT

What lessons, good and bad, can we learn from Jonah? What attitudes prevent us from viewing all people with godly compassion?

Who are the "Ninevites" in your life? What would it take to run to them, not away from them?

If you had been Jonah, how would the story have ended? Why?

SESSION 3 | LEADER GUIDE

FOCUS ATTENTION

What factors determine whether we view serving God as a privilege or a burden?

- Recall that Jonah viewed his call to service as a burden because his heart wasn't right—he lacked compassion for lost people.

- When Isaiah saw a vision of God's glory, he volunteered to serve. A vision of God's greatness and glory moves us to serve Him.

EXPLORE THE TEXT

Ask a volunteer to read Isaiah 6:1-4.

These verses focus on the revelation of God's holiness to Isaiah. What's significant about the timing of Isaiah's vision? Why do you think God chose this particular time to reveal Himself to Isaiah?

- King Uzziah represented stability. Judah enjoyed forty years of peace and prosperity under his reign.

- There is a tendency toward self-reliance and moral laxity during times of economic prosperity.

- Fear and a sense of insecurity are common responses during leadership transitions, because people don't know what to expect.

What are some ways God reveals His glory to people today?

- Glory can be defined as the manifestation of God's presence, worth, and significance.

- God has revealed His glory in creation and in His Son Jesus.

- Revelation of God's glory encourages His followers to worship and honor Him.

Ask a volunteer to read Isaiah 6:5-7.

Describe the connection between how one sees God and how one responds to God. Why did Isaiah's vision shift from focusing on God's glory to realizing his own unworthiness in verse 5?

- The more Isaiah recognized God's glory, the more he recognized his own sinfulness.

- God's holiness is too profound for us to wrap our minds around. When we get a taste of it, we are humbled by our sin and aware of our dependence on Him.

What would have become of Isaiah if the story had ended with verse 5? Why do we often end our stories with feelings of inadequacy?

- We tend to think we need huge amounts of self-confidence or talent to accomplish great things for God. All we really need is an awareness of who God is and who we are in relation to Him.

- Some believers become paralyzed by feelings of unworthiness and inadequacy. God does not make us aware of His holiness and our sinfulness to make us feel ruined. He does so to prepare us to accept His forgiveness and then step up and accept opportunities to serve Him.

Ask a volunteer to read Isaiah 6:8-10.

Why did God pose a request for someone to send and not a command to go?

- God invites His followers to join Him in fulfilling His sovereign purposes.

- God wants His followers to willfully respond to His call.

Why would God send a messenger to people who weren't going to listen?

- These verses can be disturbing until we realize the Hebrew tendency is to express a consequence (refuse to listen to God) as though it were a purpose (sounds like God did not want them to listen).

- The prophet would present God's message to the people, but they would make no effort to really listen or change.

- We can never let opposition to the message or hardened unbelief be a reason for failing to be obedient to share the gospel message.

APPLY THE TEXT

How does your understanding of God's holiness compare to Isaiah's experience?

What effect should God's holy character have on the choices you make this week?

How might unconfessed sin keep us from seeing and delighting in God's glory? What do you need to confess and repent of today following Isaiah's example?

SESSION 4 | LEADER GUIDE

FOCUS ATTENTION

What is one of the most difficult assignments you've had in your professional or personal life? How did you find the ability to deal with that assignment?

- The same God who created us also calls us to serve Him. We may feel inadequate at times, but the One who made us is the One who equips us for service.

- Though Jeremiah felt inadequate for his task, God prepared His prophet to do what He called him to do.

EXPLORE THE TEXT

Ask a volunteer to read Jeremiah 1:4-6.

How did Jeremiah recognize God's call to a specific ministry?

- Jeremiah heard the "word of the Lord" that not only confirmed what God called him to do, but also answered his objections.

- Jeremiah did not ignore the objections he had to God's calling; he faced them and listened to how God answered his objections.

What can we learn about the nature of God's calling from Jeremiah?

- God knew and chose Jeremiah before he was born. God's calling is much more than using our particular gifts or acquired skills and is bigger than whatever vocational choice we might make.

- Few things are as important as knowing the will of God for our lives as we serve Him in whatever task He has called us to. When hard times would come in Jeremiah's life, the prophet would lean on this word from the Lord.

Ask a volunteer to read Jeremiah 1:7-10.

How did God react to Jeremiah's doubts and excuses? What provisions did God make for Jeremiah despite his youth? What excuses do we make today for not serving the Lord? How does God respond to these excuses?

- God reassured and encouraged Jeremiah. God Himself would empower and strengthen Jeremiah in this assignment.

- God would direct Jeremiah to the people he needed to confront and promised His presence, even though the task was difficult and Jeremiah was fearful.

- God "touched" the prophet's mouth, filling it with the words to say, and He assured Jeremiah of his calling (see 1:9-10). God's words would be the driving force behind Jeremiah's ministry. The prophet didn't have to worry about what to say. The declarations of the Lord would be more than sufficient.

What are some specific ways God provides His people today with power to accomplish the tasks to which He calls them?

- God has provided us His Word, His Spirit, and the strength of fellow Christians to empower us to overcome our inadequacies for service.

- We can be fooled into thinking that the gospel needs help to sound current or relevant. But it's the pure, unadulterated Word of God that transforms lives.

Ask a volunteer to read Jeremiah 1:11-16.

What object lessons did God use to reassure Jeremiah? How did these lessons encourage Jeremiah that the Lord would fulfill His promise to bring judgment (which was the content of Jeremiah's message)?

- The almond tree was the first to bloom in January, meaning that the seasons were changing and promising a change to come.

- The boiling pot promised that the disaster from the north (Babylonian empire) was building, and one day Judah's sin would reach the boiling point where God would send judgment.

Ask a volunteer to read Jeremiah 1:17-19.

What would make God's message a difficult one for Jeremiah to deliver?

- Knowing his message was not one that people wanted to hear must have been quite an obstacle for Jeremiah to overcome, especially when addressing a king who had the power to imprison or execute Jeremiah.

What are some practical ways you can be prepared for confronting opposition as you stand for truth?

- Being prayerful and well-studied in the Word of God will give us confidence, especially knowing that it is God Himself who changes hearts.

APPLY THE TEXT

What are some of the obstacles that get in the way of believers living out their calling?

What reassurances from the life of Jeremiah would help you move forward in faith toward what God has called you to do?

SESSION 5 | LEADER GUIDE

FOCUS ATTENTION

Do you have an alarm system on your house or car? When has it scared someone away? When has it failed to work? Has it ever given false alarms?

- Discuss the importance of making sure alarm systems work properly.
- God's people were captives in Babylon because they failed to heed His warnings in the past. God faithfully continued sending prophets like Ezekiel to warn them.

EXPLORE THE TEXT

Ask a volunteer to read Ezekiel 33:1-9.

What do we learn from verses 1-7 about the role of a watchman in ancient Israel? What could happen if the watchman didn't perform his job?

- The watchman took his post on the city walls and scanned the horizon for approaching enemies. If the watchman did not fulfill his duties, he left the city vulnerable to attack and destruction.

In what ways was Ezekiel to serve as a watchman (vv. 7-9)? What was the specific responsibility for which God would judge Ezekiel?

- Ezekiel's assigned task of watching and warning was spiritual rather than physical.
- The prophet was held responsible for obediently sharing God's message, not for the response of the people. Similar to a watchman on a city wall, he could not force residents to believe his report.

Ask a volunteer to read Ezekiel 33:10-11.

What was the Lord's response to the people in verse 11? What does it reveal about God's character?

- God provided a way for the exiles to have a new relationship with Him and to find new life. He revealed His mercy, willingness to forgive, and persistent love to the exiles.
- While God had every right to condemn them for their sin, He never brought judgment without first warning.

For what is God blamed in our day? How do these "accusations" hold up in light of verses 10-11?

- The people in Ezekiel's day mistakenly believed God enjoyed judging them and watching them suffer. In our culture, some blame God when things go wrong or they face difficulties. God is loving, not capricious.

- God longs for His people to choose life instead of death (see Deut. 30:11-20).

Ask a volunteer to read Ezekiel 33:30-33.

Where and why were people talking about Ezekiel? Why were they coming to hear him preach?

The good news in verses 30-33 was that the people were flocking to hear Ezekiel. What was the bad news?

- While Ezekiel was drawing large numbers, few (if any) of the exiles truly were seeking to hear from the Lord. They came to see the celebrity, the "singer of love songs."

- Ezekiel's audience wanted to be entertained. They saw Ezekiel as a performer on a stage.

Why do you think these people listened to Ezekiel's words but didn't change their ways? What do these verses tell us God values most?

- Ezekiel's preaching had not yet penetrated the hearts of his audience. They came out of curiosity and appreciated Ezekiel's entertainment value.

- We do not please God merely by hearing His warning, believing His promises, or enjoying a good worship service. We please God when we obey His Word.

APPLY THE TEXT

In what sense are we the watchmen for our communities and cities? How is being watchful related to sharing the gospel?

For what reasons do Christians often resist the role of watchmen?

What are some practical ways you can be "on watch" this week?

SESSION 6 | LEADER GUIDE

FOCUS ATTENTION

When have you had to deliver a difficult message? How did it go? How did the recipient(s) receive the message?

- Malachi described his message as a "pronouncement" (v. 1). The Hebrew word suggests a burden or heavy message containing stern warnings or judgment. Malachi truly had a burden from the Lord he needed to share with the Israelites.

- Many of Malachi's hearers received his message with cynicism and scorn. A small number remained faithful to the Lord and receptive to the prophet's message.

EXPLORE THE TEXT

Ask a volunteer to read Malachi 1:1-2.

The Lord begins this book with a declaration of His love. How did God reassure the people of His love? What does this say about God's love for us?

- God pointed out that the people doubted His love for them.

- "I loved Jacob" (v. 2) refers to God's choosing him over Esau as the recipient of His blessing. God reminded the Israelites that His choosing them—even when there was nothing worthy about them—was evidence of His love.

- God's love for us is due to His grace, not our goodness (see Eph. 1:4-6).

Ask a volunteer to read Malachi 1:6-8.

What did God call Himself (besides "Lord of Hosts") in verse 6? To whom was He speaking? What was God saying by using these metaphors?

- God referred to Himself as a "father" and a "master."

- God spoke to the priests who despised His name. He established His authority over the priests. They should have obeyed Him.

How did the priests in Malachi's day despise God's name? What did they offer to God that they wouldn't dare offer to their governor? What warning can we find in this for our own lives?

- The priests were allowing the people to offer blind, lame animals as sacrifices.

- They would never think of giving their governor less than their best. They did, however, sacrifice to God blind, crippled, and diseased animals.

- We sometimes give our work, our hobbies, and our friends the best we have in time and effort, but give God only a small token of our life's resources. God wants our first and our best.

Ask a volunteer to read Malachi 1:9-11.

Look at verses 9-10. What was God's response to the sacrifices of His people? What would God rather have happen if the people continued to give less than their best?

- God said He would not show His people favor.

- The Lord would rather have the temple doors closed and the sacrifices stopped.

What does verse 11 say about God? In light of what it says about Him, what does it affirm about the priests?

- One day even Gentiles everywhere will recognize the greatness of God and worship Him. (This is repeated in verse 14.)

- God's own people failed to see the greatness of God. This verse affirms the greatness of God and the smallness of the priests.

Ask a volunteer to read Malachi 1:12-14.

According to verse 13, how did the priests feel about offering sacrifices? How can we apply this to our own worship?

- They felt that offering sacrifices was a nuisance.

- This should cause us to examine our motives for worshiping and serving God. Are we here because we love God? Are we here out of duty, out of habit? God sees into the deepest recesses of our hearts and examines our motives.

Do you think people today try to "con" or deceive God? Explain.

- The worshiper in verse 14 said one thing to God but then did another. He is called a "deceiver." He was only deceiving himself, thinking He could get away with giving God less than his best.

- God is the great King of the universe. He knows our hearts and deserves our best.

APPLY THE TEXT

What does your attitude toward worship say about your relationship with God?

In what ways can you honor God with your life and demonstrate wholehearted love for Him?

Then I heard
the voice of the Lord asking:
Who should I send?
Who will go for us?
I said:
Here I am.
Send me.

ISAIAH 6:8

Whether you're a new Christian or you have believed in Jesus for several years, the people of the Bible have so much wisdom to offer. For that reason, we have created additional resources for churches that want to maximize the reach and impact of the *Characters* studies.

Complete Series Leader Pack

Want to take your group through the whole *Explore the Bible: Characters* series? You'll want a *Complete Series Leader Pack*. This *Pack* includes *Leader Kits* from Volume 1 - Volume 7. It allows you to take your group from The Patriarchs all the way to The Early Church Leaders.

$179.99

Video Bundle for Groups

All video sessions are available to purchase as a downloadable bundle.

$60.00

eBooks

A digital version of the *Bible Study Book* is also available for those who prefer studying with a phone or tablet. Some churches also find eBooks easier to distribute to study participants.

Starter Packs

You can save money and time by purchasing starter packs for your group or church. Every *Church Starter Pack* includes a digital *Church Launch Kit* and access to a digital version of the *Leader Kit* videos.

$99.99 | **Single Group Starter Pack**
(10 *Bible Study Books*, 1 *Leader Kit*)

$449.99 | **Small Church Starter Pack**
(50 *Bible Study Books*, 5 *Leader Kit* DVDs, and access to video downloads)

$799.99 | **Medium Church Starter Pack**
(100 *Bible Study Books*, 10 *Leader Kit* DVDs, and access to video downloads)

$3495.99 | **Large Church Starter Pack**
(500 *Bible Study Books*, 50 *Leader Kit* DVDs, and access to video downloads)

LifeWay.com/characters
Order online or call 800.458.2772.

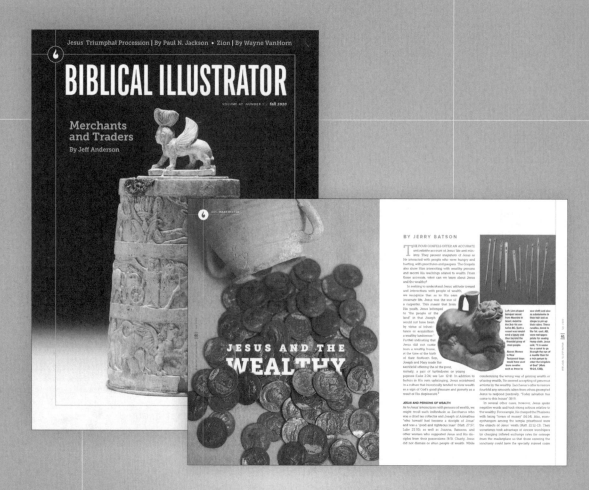

WANT TO KNOW EVEN MORE ABOUT BIBLICAL CHARACTERS?

The *Explore the Bible: Characters* series features information from the pages of *Biblical Illustrator*. And there are more insights on the way. Every quarter, you'll find remarkable content that will greatly enhance your study of the Bible:

- Fascinating photographs, illustrations, maps, and archaeological finds
- Informative articles on biblical lands, people, history, and customs
- Insights about how people lived, learned, and worshiped in biblical times

Order at lifeway.com/biblicalillustrator or call 800.458.2772.

Continue Your
Exploration

---- **VOLUME 5** ----
JESUS

Studying the characters of the Bible helps us understand how God works in the world, loves His people, and moves through His people to accomplish His plans. The next volume of *Explore the Bible: Characters* focuses exclusively on God's Son, Jesus—His teachings, miracles, crucifixion, and more.

Bible Study Book 005823507 **$9.99**
Leader Kit 005823540 **$29.99**

EXPLORE YOUR OPTIONS

EXPLORE THE BIBLE.

EXPLORE THE BIBLE

If you want to understand the Bible in its historical, cultural, and biblical context, few resources offer the thoroughness of the Explore the Bible ongoing quarterly curriculum. Over the course of nine years, you can study the whole truth, book by book, in a way that's practical, sustainable, and age appropriate for your entire church.

6- TO 8-WEEK STUDIES

If you're looking for short-term resources that are more small-group friendly, visit the LifeWay website to see Bible studies from a variety of noteworthy authors, including Ravi Zacharias, J.D. Greear, Matt Chandler, David Platt, Tony Evans, and many more.

Prices and availability subject to change without notice.